The

BOOK

of

KNOWING

and

WORTH

Jeremy P. Tarcher/Penguin
a member of Penguin Group (USA)
New York

The

BOOK

of

KNOWING

and

WORTH

A CHANNELED TEXT

PAUL SELIG

JEREMY P. TARCHER/PENGUIN
Published by the Penguin Group
Penguin Group (USA) LLC
375 Hudson Street
New York, New York 10014

USA · Canada · UK · Ireland · Australia
New Zealand · India · South Africa · China

penguin.com
A Penguin Random House Company

Most Tarcher/Penguin books are available at special quantity discounts for
bulk purchase for sales promotions, premiums, fund-raising, and educational
needs. Special books or book excerpts also can be created to fit specific needs.
For details, write: Special.Markets@us.penguingroup.com.

Library of Congress Cataloging-in-Publication Data

The book of knowing and worth : a channeled text / Paul Selig
p.   cm.
ISBN 978-0-399-16610-5
1. Spirit writings.   I. Selig, Paul.
BF1301.B555   2013   2013036562
133.9′3—dc23

Printed in the United States of America
7   9   10   8   6

Book design by Meighan Cavanaugh

CONTENTS

PREFACE

This book is the third and, in some respects, the most significant of the channeled teachings brought through Paul Selig. It is dramatically practical and clarifying—probably the most complete and well-rounded channeled spiritual psychology since the work of Edgar Cayce in the first half of the twentieth century.

In the recent history of channeled literature—from Cayce to Jane Roberts and the Seth material to Helen Schucman and *A Course in Miracles*—it is possible to detect an intimate and important connection between the channeler and the intelligence that speaks through him or her. Paul's messages arrive from a consortium of unseen "Guides," whose voices are deeply ethical, penetratingly insightful regarding the foibles of human nature, and unsparingly blunt about the possibilities and pitfalls facing us in the present era. As an intellect, Paul, too, possesses these qualities and serves as a fine instrument—a kind of Stradivarius of the soul—through which the Guides can play their notes.

This same quality of relationship, though with different tones and elements, appeared in the interplay between Edgar Cayce and his "Source." The nature of Cayce as a man fundamentally colored the tenor of the communication that came through him. Cayce was a Christian mystic, a person of Southern agrarian roots, and a dedicated reader of the King James Bible. These qualities lent color and voice to the channeled energies that traversed him. Paul, by contrast, is a lifelong urban dweller, a university teacher and widely produced playwright, and a contemporary man accustomed to a world in which spiritual choices and psychological vernacular abound. These qualities, in turn, mark the tone found in Paul's twenty-first-century teachings. Yet beyond the skin-deep differences, Paul's work, like Cayce's, resounds with a set of universal religious ethics, a deep respect for the individual and for individual identity, and a psychological depth that allows each reader to see his or her own personal questions, crises, and hopes in this material. The work of Paul and the Guides is spiritual literature of great substance and posterity.

I began publishing Paul's work with the Guides in 2010, shortly after meeting him at a conference for independent scholars of religion at the Esalen Institute. This conference, held in the spring of 2009, marked Paul's initial public acknowledgment of his work as a medium and channel. Until then, his academic appointments at New York University's Tisch School of the Arts, where he teaches dramatic writing, and at Goddard College, where he directs the MFA program, made him conservative about disclosing the more occult aspects of his life. The unanimity of praise among conference attendees encouraged Paul to continue the public phase of his channeling, and in the summer of 2010, his first channeled book, *I Am the Word*, appeared from Tarcher/Penguin. A new work, *The Book of Love and Creation*, followed in 2012. In the brief time since then, I have watched Paul's work enter foreign translations and grow in impact around the world.

The expanding popularity of Paul's work is remarkable on several counts. While the viewpoint of Paul's Guides is very much in harmony with tenets of New Thought and the ideals of the human-potential movement, the Guides do not offer a narrowly conceived message of personal attainment or self-enrichment. The Guides do not eschew such aims, but their teaching requires a concurrent growth of self-understanding and personal observation on the part of the individual; it demands the cultivation of empathy and inner study; and it often offers rigorous exercises in these pursuits. This teaching is not for people who are easily distracted or narrowly self-interested. It places a demand on the whole person.

This is not to say the teaching lacks encouragement, hope, and portent. The Guides repeatedly state that if the reader employs their affirmations—and in this book the keynote is "I know who I am, I know what I am, I know how I serve"—the Guides will offer invisible assistance and will aid the individual's development. The individual's ability to receive this help rests—as with any authentic spiritual program—on his or her depth of hunger for self-change. If that hunger is sincere, so the Guides promise, their helping energies will be felt, and immediately so.

This teaching places us at a remarkable precipice: Its spreading influence reflects a new phase of maturity in the therapeutic spiritual philosophy that often goes under the term "New Age." This channeled wisdom signals both a cultural turning point and, quite possibly, an individual turning point for each of its readers. It places us at the front of a rigorous and hopeful spiritual expression, and a methodology for self-change.

—MITCH HOROWITZ
May 31, 2013

The following are transcripts of channeling sessions that were recorded in New York City between November 22, 2012, and April 11, 2013. Paul Selig served as the channel. Victoria Nelson was present via telephone from Berkeley, California. Two sessions were conducted in Port Townsend, Washington, when Paul and Victoria were present in the same room during the channeling, and two more were recorded during Paul's Thursday night group, with Victoria attending by phone.

INTRODUCTION

Day One

We are speaking as we can about what is to come and what must be said to illumine those who read this text. This is a time of great change and transition, and each of you who stands in your own worth will align to your own knowing and claim your identity in the highest way available to you now. This is a time of great change and a great awakening is upon you, but you must attend to yourselves as the one who is responsible for your own identity. And we underline this: *You must be responsible to yourself as the one responsible for your own identity.*

The claims that you make, each one of you, "I know who I am in my life, in my work, in my gatherings, in my exchanges," are the ways you identify yourself with. And what we must tell you now is that when you operate in a diminished sense of self, you operate in lack and in fear. You have not been told who you were and, consequently, you identify yourself through structures that adhere to limitations.

Now each one of you reading this has already woken to the fact that there is more to this world than what you have thought. You are allowing the new experience to come to you in your own identity as a new possibility unveils itself. And as you do this, you create a new possibility, a new possibility to be, to see the world differently, and to adhere to new possibilities as they may present themselves. So you are already ready. You are already preparing yourselves for the new ideals that are coming to you through the acquisition of the information that we will present to you in this volume of knowing. And that is the title of this book: *The Book of Knowing and Worth*. Now we say this again, *The Book of Knowing and Worth* will be the title for this text because it is about your own knowing, and the claim of worth that is inherited by each of you as you sing your song on this plane and lift this plane of existence to a new level of incarnation.

What is happening now on this plane is that those of you who have gathered have decided to incarnate at the highest level available to you, and the acquisition of knowing of who and what you truly are is what is required to make this so. When there is a mass elevation in consciousness, what begins to happen is that the incarnations that you stand in begin to align to the next phase of development on this plane and the plane must shift itself to reflect the new knowing that each of you are born into.

Now you have questions about this. "What does my world look like?" "Who am I at this next level of incarnation?" And we will tell you who you are, each and every one of you: The aspect of the Divine that you are and have always been intended to be has come forward to be renamed: *"I know who I am, I know what I am, I know how I serve."* And the claim of this, as you create from it, expressed as you, culminates in a new awakening of your own being through the manifestation of the self as the Christ.

Now we don't mean this in a heretical way. We mean this in the most truthful way available to you. The aspect of the Creator that may be manifested in form is how we talk of the Christ. And the Christ *as you, as you, as you* is the teaching of this text. Can man be Christ? Man is Christ but has not awakened to it. The awakening that we speak of is the inheritance of the Creator born in each and every individual awakened to his own worth, to her own worth, as a manifestation of the Creator in form.

You stand in your worth each and every day. Like it or not, you decide what you are worth. You always have. "I am a small man with fear." "I am a happy lady with three children, I know who I am when I go to school to drop them off and go back and make my cookies." You claim your identities, large and small, in your worth. And you only claim your worth as you feel you are allowed to. You have been diminished, as we have taught you in our previous texts, by structures that would keep you in fear of claiming this. And we are singing your song today for you so that you may learn the words to the song of your own soul's significance.

"I know who I am, I know what I am, I know how I serve. And as I sing, I know. And as I know, I incarnate as my true self. And the true self I speak of is the Christ in manifestation as man."

We sing your song for you so that you may learn the words. We know who you are, we know what you are intended to be. But you must design yourselves, each and every one of you, to the awareness that this can be so, that you may claim yourselves, each and every one of you, as you have been meant to be.

Now you decide, you decide, you decide every waking moment of your life who and what you are. "I am the man who is ashamed." "I am the woman who laughs." "I am the one who brings joy." "I am the one who worries too much." However you say yourselves as your claim, you incarnate as. And your incarnation, we say, is the level of vibration that you attend to in your worth.

You are worth what you say you are. You always have been. If you say you are worth two dollars, you will call yourself two dollars; you will claim two dollars and not a penny more. When you know you are the Christ, the aspect of the Creator that may be in form, by the level of knowing and design and creation that is available at that level of consciousness, you claim your identity in a new way and your world, your world, your world will reflect this.

Now Paul is wondering, are we telling mankind that they

are the Christ? And yes, we are. But you have not known the magnificence of who and what you are because you have not been attuned to the possibility that it can be so. It has been made so already. The way was shown to you many times, but what you have done as a civilization is adhere to paradigms that will tell you this cannot be so. You relinquish your authority, you each relinquish your authority every time that you agree that you are small, that you are dominated by a structure that must know more than you.

You design this, you know. You are so used to this, to playing the game of limitation that you create from it. It is the hat you wear that shields you from the sun that would awaken you. "I know who I am in my limitation, in my poverty, in my fear, in my shame, in my unknowing."

Now you may know things. You may claim your knowing but you must do this in an awareness of your worth. Your worth, we say, is what is at stake here, and it is the teaching of this text. We do not design a text to make you feel better about yourselves, that is not our interest. However, it is helpful if you feel good because you will be more attentive. But when we say we want you knowing, we want you knowing of your worth in a profound way.

"I have a right to live my life in an awareness of my Christed Self in my manifestation and call to me those experiences, those expressions of the Christ that would meet me at this level of knowing."

Now you decide, you the reader, the listener, the witness to this expression on a page, on a page, on a page that is informed by *knowing.* And the information we give you on the page is being endowed with properties and claims that will transition you from the small self you have known into the manifestation of the Christ as can be born in man. *Do you know this?* The Christ can be born in man, in each of you, and in the ones beside you, in the ones you may meet and may never meet. It can be born because this is the time of the Creator's welcome to each of you.

Now we sing your song for you in this text so that you may learn the words, so that you may get comfortable with the ideals that we set forth for you to adhere to. The designs you make, the way you move through this incarnation that have been born in worry and designed in fear will begin to unfold. They will begin to peel back so you may see yourselves as you are intended to be. The designs that we give you, the ways that you may know yourselves in conjunction with your fellows and all the things you have created will be what you know in a new way as you respond to our teaching.

Now we ask you this: Who is frightened of the possibility of being the Christ? As being manifested as the Christ consciousness as can be attained in the bodies you stand in, in the awareness you may hold? Who among you is frightened of this? You all are, you know, and do you know why? Because you were lied to and you were told it could not be so. Now when we say it is so, we say it from expression, from our knowing, from our being as we incarnate as this, we say it can be so.

Now we have known ourselves in different ways, in different forms, at different times in this history, in this ideal you call a plane. As we come to teach you, we have taken material form, or we have stayed in identity in the ethers. It does not matter. But what we can claim for you is that this is so, has been so, and you were lied to that it could not be so.

We pull back the pages of the book that was held from you to show you the real words that are imprinted on the page. And the real words imprinted on the page, *I Am the Word: The Book of Knowing and Worth,* will call to you your identity in every expression you know.

Everything you see before you, everything you see, you have agreed to. Do you know this? Everything on the shelf of your cabinets, everything on the street, everything in the sky you have agreed to. It could not be there if it was not agreed to by you collectively *and* individually we will say, because the individual is an aspect of the collective whole.

Now we say to you: What you witness, what you have created and are in agreement with, you are shaking hands with. When you agree with something, you shake its hand and you are in alignment with it. What you are in alignment with, you concur with, you are in co-resonance as. What you are in co-resonance as, you hold as your frequency. What you hold as your frequency you manifest.

As we say you are the Christ, you must remember yourselves and release the acquisitions, the claims of self, the things you co-resonate with that are not in alignment with this truth.

And those things that are not in alignment will be released for you by the reading of this text. We have a mission here that those of you who decide, and we underline *decide*, that this can be so, will have the experience that is intended by this text. Those of you who decide that you may align, that you may be in triumph, that you may be risen as the Christ manifested in man, will have the experience, and the knowing, and the absolution of your history as one in limitation that may be claimed at this juncture, at your time.

The time that you stand in now is a time of judgment and reckoning. And we do not use hierarchical terms to clarify this for you. You are the Creator. You face your own creations, and when you face a creation, you decide what you must do next. The time that you stand in is one of a reckoning. A reckoning is a witnessing and a facing so you may align to a new possibility.

The awakening of each man as he stands in his body knowing himself as truth, as an incarnation of an aspect of the Creator that may be known as him in his worth, is what we sing to you. We bring on each page a teaching that may be known by the mind. We bring on each page a teaching that may be known by the spirit. We bring on each page a teaching that may be known by the soul as the personality transitions into this new level of awareness: "I know who I am, I know what I am, I know how I serve."

Who you are, we say, is who you say you are. Understand this please. *Who you are is what you say you are.* "I am an aspect of the Creator in form" is a claim of worth and truth. You will always be this, you have always been this, it cannot be otherwise. What you are is in this body, in this expression, in this life you have chosen to bring yourself this experience. How you serve, we say, how each man serves, how each being serves is how they are expressed as their own consciousness—what they agree to, what they agree to and shake hands, what they co-resonate with and create from. When you know how you serve, you know who you are and your reflection is brought back to you in manifestation. And this means you get what you expect and you expect to get what you know.

When you know who you are in truth, your life will change because it cannot not change. Do you understand this, yes? You cannot go to the store and pick the peas off the shelf and expect them to be other when you get home. You go to the peas, you get the peas. You go to the manifestation of yourself as the Christ, as the being who can be incarnated as the Christ and you witness it in everything around you. You do because you can, and you can because you know, and what you know is what you claim.

There is no one reading this text who does not know this already on a very deep level. You are born with this information. It has been instilled in you by God, if you wish, by what creates you, as you, to be remembered as you as the aspect of Source. But then you were lied to and you agree with the lie. The lie has been going on for far too long.

Now we understand that the humanity you hold is many

faceted. You have your feelings, you have your bodies, you have these things that were inherited by you in structure, in form, in governance, in religion that inform everything. But we are telling you this now: *You are not your history.* You are not your history and, in fact, you never were intended to be. But the walls that were forged between you and your Divine Self were cemented by information that was historically born to keep you from your true worth. You can no longer blame anybody for being who and what you are. All you do now is re-create what you have known in limitation because it's all you think you're allowed to get.

Now we ask you a question: Do you want this? If you want it, you must keep reading and you must *do* this book as if it is a course in your own awakening to the Christ as you. If you do not want this, we thank you for your patience so far and we say, one day we will nod to you, we will welcome you again and, perhaps, we will be in conversation because you are not ready yet to release what you have known. But when you are, this information will be available to you both in the material form and in the spiritual dictation that aligns to the text on the page. There is no one reading this book who is not ready to know these things once again.

Now we ask you this: What stands in the way of your worth? What have you created that would keep you from God? What have you attended to, believed, agreed upon, that would keep you from the love of your Creator? What are those things that you have invested so much power in that they would keep you in hiding from the kingdom that is welcoming you? You must look at these things and realize what they are: creations born in fear that you use now to protect you from the possibility that you may be much more wonderful than you have ever imagined.

We sing your song for you, and we sing it now. The aspect of you that is ready to be welcomed will be sung as a note on a violin. It will strain, it will play out, it will echo into the universe and call you back to yourself as your music plays. When you are in resonance with the Christ, when the note is being sung and played as you, and we underline *as, as* you, you will sing the song of the Christ and your identity will be healed:

"I know who I am, I know what I am, I know how I serve."

"I know who I am" is a claim of truth. You always know who you are, even when you think you don't. What you claim as you is how you manifest and what you call to you.

As your incarnation makes itself known to you, what you would welcome to you will be in transition, and the high forms that would present themselves to you in this knowing will be claimed as you say, "Welcome." The knowing of what you are, "I know who I am, I know *what* I am"—and we underline *what*—the manifestation that you stand in—will always be true. You know what you have, you know what you create because it is expressed by you in this material form. How you serve is how you express. And every one of you is singing his song, her song, in expression every moment of every waking day. Your vibration is your song and your vibration is reflected as your consciousness.

You cannot think a thing and not align to it. The thought is what aligns you. The broadcast you play as the radio you are is your expression. If you do not like the radio station that you are expressing, it is time to change the channel, and we are giving you the tools to do that.

The awakening that will come to you, to each one who responds to this text as a teaching, will bring you to a new awareness not only of your worth, but of the worth of all your fellows, of every living thing, of all that you have created. The manifestations will be such that you may no longer expect yourself to know yourself as you were, because who you were was a product of thought and agreement to structure that no longer aligns to you. When it no longer aligns to you, it is not in your frequency. What is not in your frequency cannot be created in manifestation in the physical realm. Do you each understand this? The significance of this teaching as we attend to you is that you must realize who the heck you are, and what you know, and how you may be expressed to the world will be in wonder.

Now we have spoken of wonder in our previous texts, and when you wonder, you open to a new possibility; nothing can happen anew without a new possibility first being presented. You must open to the possibility in order to change what you have known. This is the awakening. We are saying yes to you, to each of you, to each one of you as you say yes to yourselves:

"I know who I am in my worth, I know what I am in my worth, I know how I serve in my worth."

And the song that is sung by you is one of many songs as the great chorus ensues and the new awakening comes and this plane is healed of fear.

Now we ask you this: If you do not want to go on this journey, why? You must learn to ask yourself the right questions. Why do you wish to go on this journey and why do you not? You must become accountable for each choice you make. Because if you are not accountable, you are not aware, and if you are not aware, you are asleep. We wake you up to your own choices, to the one who may choose, who may sing, who may redesign herself and, consequently, redesign her world in the highest way that you may be in alignment to.

The song has begun! The orchestra is prepared! The music is open to be read! And the vibration is high! We sing with you now! We welcome you to the new text, to the new adventure in your worth, to all that may be called to you and all that will be left behind! We sing your song with you, and together we join the world in its awakening.

We thank you for your presence. We will speak to you soon. Good night.

I

I KNOW WHO I AM

Day Two

Why do you worry that there will be no transmission when there has never *not* been a transmission in all the time we have worked with you?[1] You must learn to trust the authors of this text to get their own needs met through this interaction. While we are not impatient with you, we come prepared, and we come prepared to teach the students of our work what they may need to know to learn who they are and what they must do to stand in their worth.

The lives you live, the lives all of you live, have been predicated by history that is coming to an end. And we say "to an end" in a good way. The lives you have known that you have decided upon and aligned to were created for you to fulfill an experience, and the experience that was fulfilled has brought

---

1 This is being directed to Paul, who had expressed concern prior to the session.

you to where you stand today; where you stand today in all of your creations, in all you have agreed to, shaken hands with and claimed.

Now the new day, the new time, the new belief that you can hold this vibration is what will claim you and move you forward. And as we teach you this, we agree to a new light, and a new light is the anchoring of the Christ in manifestation in this plane as you each agree to become it.

Now how can there be many Christs? How could there not be? If the Creator that is you is incarnating as you, this must be available to everybody. You cannot have one light in the darkness to illumine the world. There must be many lights, and so in fact there are. The designs you have, the designs you hold as your energy fields have been created to demonstrate this. And the demonstration of this, the alignment to this is where we wish to take you. The hunger you hold in your souls to be remembered, to be held again in the body of All is what is being agreed to.

Now you align yourselves to everything you know. That is always the truth. "I know it is Monday," you align to Monday. "I know it is Tuesday," you align to Tuesday. You agree to Tuesday, so you go to work on Tuesday and on and on and on. How you agree is based in cultural dictates that were created for you at different times in history. And you all said, "Okay. We will go to work, it is a Tuesday." And on Tuesday you go. You have not given permission yet to re-create paradigms that have been so enforced you agree to them without question, without thinking twice. "It's noon I must have my coffee." "It is my wedding night, I must make love." Whatever you claim in agreement to a structure is what you choose.

Now today we are doing something new. We are going to defy a structure that you have inherited for ten minutes of our teaching. And then we will talk about it. How you know yourselves has been inherited by you because you were told your name. It was printed on a piece of paper when you were born, and you say, "That must be who I am" as you learned the name aloud and responded to it. How you know yourselves outside of your name is your frequency. And as we re-identify with you as your frequency, we align you outside of the name you have held.

Now, the frequency you hold is a great being. It is a great emission of your consciousness that aligns to the truth of who you are because it can never not be separate from it. The designs you hold in separation are born in personality. And the personality self who recognizes separation aligns to all things separate and dismisses the possibility that the questions that you may be asking yourselves about your design could take you to any place else than you have ever known.

What we will do with you now is take you outside of your history. Take you outside of the name you were born with and take you to a new place of creation. On the count of three what we are going to do is move the frequency of this text to align you to a new creation. And the creation we align you to is yourself in love, as love, with love and in accordance with all the love that is.

Now as we say one, two, three, we install in each of you the ammunition to charge yourselves with this creation. As you are charged by this creation, you claim it, it is inherited as you and you align to it in your subconscious mind. Once the subconscious mind is aligned to a new creation, there is a process of engaging it as it is claimed in manifestation. The design that you hold is being responded to by our texts. And our text is a creation of love implied and impressed as you, as you claim, as you align and you accept and receive. Now we do this with you each:

One. Two. Three.

What we are doing with you right now is shifting the vibration you have known as yourself to a template, a new template that will withstand change. As love cannot be changed in its infinite self, it always recognizes its worth. And those things that you would claim as yourself that are no longer in accordance with love will melt away, will lift away, will be taken from you as if a great wind comes to carry the debris of your history far from you.

Now the permission we need from you to make this so is an agreement with yourself that you can align to this possibility. And in the alignment to the possibility you agree to become your intention: "I know who I am, I know what I am, I know how I serve."

The agreement you are making now is to align yourself and

your history to a new creation. If the history is no longer in alignment with the vibration we hold, the history will be released in such a way that it does not temper your expression in harm. It only lets you know yourselves in the face of your changes as one who may grow and change.

We distinguish one thing for you now: As we say you are not your history, we do not tell you that the history did not occur. So you are not blaming your history for where you stand today, you are simply agreeing that you are not your history and you may step forward and claim the new creation that is you in manifestation.

As we align you each, as we recognize you each in the new template, "I know who I am, what I am, how I serve," we agree with you. And our agreement with you is that we will not leave you on the roadside, we will not pass you by, we will not forget that you agreed to sing this song that we teach you. As long as you remember your name, your true self, "I know who I am, I know what I am, I know how I serve," we will work with you to actualize yourselves as the truest creation you may embody as.

As we use the term "Christ," we understand that many of you have issue with the word because your history precludes you from receiving the true message of it. As we speak of the Christ we create a new ideal as you, actualized as you. The actualization as you as an aspect of the Creator in her knowing and embodiment, in his expression and being, is the Christ in manifestation as man. Now the decisions you have made up until now that this could not be so are being responded already, by us, as you work with this text. We have said in the past that the text operates on different levels, the text on the page and then the true imprinting of vibration that lives within each page that calls to you the expression and the vibration that we saw through as we align you to your possibility of manifestation.

As you agree to read, you also agree to align. If you can imagine reading a book while there is music playing, this will be the easiest example for you. As you read the words on the page, the music commences and it informs you, and your whole vibration is aligned to the music that is gifted to you as you partake in this teaching.

The creations you have known up until today have been made by you to know yourselves, to decide for yourselves that you may be on this journey. So we ask you to thank them all, to thank everything in your life up until now, every piece of heart, every piece of pain, every joy, every love, every thought that has brought you to this moment. Our choice for you is to hear you as you sing, and as you sing you lift, and as you lift you agree to align to your true self: "I know who I am, I know what I am, I know how I serve."

Now the title of this chapter, "I Know Who I Am," is what we will teach you now. The self that you have known and pretended to be operates in illusion. She has her job, or her family, or the ways of self-identifying through the creations she has made. But what she does not know is her infinite self, because the infinite self has not been aligned to a new possibility outside of the responses that she has agreed that she can hold. If you are told to laugh at a funny movie, you go in an expectation of laughter. If you go to grieve at a funeral, you expect to shed tears. The conditioned responses you have known yourself through, in many ways, give you an appearance of choice, but in fact they have been chosen for you.

Now we are not denying your humanity. We are celebrating it. And we are all for laughter and we accept the tears as part of your life, but we do not tell you when you should express them. As you are pointed in a direction by your history, "this happens and you must feel that way," you begin to know yourself through those expressions. When enough of you agree to something, it becomes solidified in material form. And the creations that surround you now, each one of you, have been agreed upon by you all.

Now the new level of response that we would offer you, "I know who I am," does not preclude laughter or tears. It sings a new song that rises above conditioned behavior so you may be responding to what is true and not to what is not true, not to what you have been taught to believe must be so because you all agreed upon it for so long. "I know who I am" is a claim of worth. When you know who you are at a true level, "I know I am an aspect of the Creator in form, I am manifested as such," that begins to be your expression.

As you vibrate in accord with that, what is around you begins to move, to transform to recognize the new creation that you claim as your frequency. The vibrations that you hold, each and every one of you, are chosen by you in several ways. Your emotional selves, the ideas you hold, the choices you make born in your thinking all inform your vibration.

As you align to the Christ as your true self, "I know who I am, I know what I am, I know how I serve," you decide anew that this is you in manifestation. As we said yesterday, who you are is who you say you are, and your dominion always is claimed by you with this intention. You are in resonance with your claim of truth, and your expression directs it to you as a response to what you have stated.

Now when you claim, "I know what I am," you are also making a decision. To know what you are means to know who and what you are in this incarnation, in the body you stand in, and how you are expressed in all of the things you see around you, the mass that you hold as your body, the things that you see before you that reflect that, that adhere to the makings of your expression on this plane. "I know what I am" is that claim.

How you serve, we say, how anybody serves, is how they are expressed as consciousness. And you must understand this very simply: As you are always in vibration, you are always in expression, regardless of what you think. Your vibration is your life in manifestation. It is what holds things to you; it is what repels things as well. The vibration that you hold is how you serve.

As you are expressed as your true self, your vibration is transformed, and your service, as we say, is how you express this in all areas of your being. Now you design your lives in accordance with mandates that you have been taught. "How I

serve must be something I do that is nice for other people because that is how I know service to be." And you are welcome
to do that and, in fact, you may be called, but what we are telling you is something quite different.

When you align to the Christ as the vibration that you hold,
that is what you express and that is your service, because what
you call to you in response to this will be in alignment with
that level of knowing and creation. Now we will explain this for
you. When you move into a high consciousness and your vibration is in accord with that, the manifestations on this plane
must be altered to reflect the new level of awareness and the
new level of expression that you have claimed. In this claim you
call things to you, and what you claim to you must be in alignment with this new ideal. It cannot be otherwise. Do you understand this, please? It cannot be otherwise.

What you would claim to yourselves at this new level of
consciousness must be in accord with it, and what is in accord
with the Christ as a manifestation must be in healing and is in
service. The vibration that you hold is service because you are
always expressing your vibration. So that is how you experience yourselves.

Now Paul is getting in the way. "Do we have to tell them
they are going to go and be a nurse if they are in service?" Absolutely not. For one man to be in service as himself is to be
realized as his truest self. As this man is realized as his truest
self, he is expressed as this and that is what he calls to him. He
demonstrates this in every aspect of his life because he cannot

not demonstrate it. What he is demonstrating will be love, will be the expression of the Christ, because that is how the Christ expresses itself.

Now we have to tell you something very important, because there is confusion here for many of you. Many of you believe that if you manifest as your higher self, or your Christed Self, the Christed Self is what is there for you as you wish it. And it is the opposite.

You all believe that you are in control of this on a level of ego and personality when, in fact, the opposite is true. When John demonstrates the Christ, when Mary demonstrates the Christ, it is not John as the Christ or Mary as the Christ, it is the Christ as John and Mary. The hand doesn't hold the glass. The glass, the chalice of the Christ, holds the man. Do you understand the difference, yes?

So as the Christ becomes you, and aligns those aspects of you that are in distortion, that are in fear, that are in blame, that are in heresy against the true self, the knowing of the true self comes forward and claims her purview. John as the Christ, yes. The Christ as John is much more true.

Now there is a difference, you see, because you like to be the one in authority, and in fact, you always are and you always will be. But what aspect of you, what aspect of you, what aspect of you is claiming the authority of your life? If it is John who works at a bank and has an unhappy marriage claiming his authority, he will be John with the unhappy marriage in au-thority. When you are the Christ as you manifested as you, that is the aspect of you that claims dominion. And what you claim as that aspect of the self will be aligned to the truth in service and in recognition of your worth.

We are trying to be very clear for you now, because you must understand these simple tenets to understand where we would like to take you. We are not losing your personality selves. You are being incorporated by your true self in such a way that you are no longer operating out of a pretend structure that you have misidentified as.

Now can this be so? Yes. Is it simple? Yes. Does the personality like this? Absolutely not. Because the personality self has a tremendous investment in deciding who and what she wants to be. Now if there is to be comfort to that aspect of the self as this transmission continues, it is the following: As the personality self is resumed by us to move into a healthy way of being expressed with the true self, the Christ as you in manifestation holding the fort, as it were, the safety that the personality holds is magnified many times.

Now when we speak of safety, we simply mean that the personality self knows it is held in love by the divine aspect of you that has come forward to claim itself as worthy of this manifestation.

The decisions that you have made up until now have brought you to this moment of a new creation. And a new creation, we will tell you, has come to sing your song for you, to be you, to align as you because it's always been the truth of who you are.

Mankind was lied to, as we said yesterday, by many men, by

many creations, by many systems, and man was controlled long enough. The deceit that man endured has left them in a predicament. You think you must hurt each other to be safe. You think you must win, one against the other, to be happy. You think you must cherish only one to be in partnership when, in fact, the whole world is your lover, and the only winner you have is your own recognition of your divine worth. Everything that stands before you and a recognition of your divine worth must be encountered and decided upon, one at a time or in groups, but it must be decided for you to be liberated.

If this was not possible we would not be your teachers. We have things we could be doing, you know, and waking up many people at one time is within our purview and brings us joy. But the manifestation of God as man is what is here to be worth, to be worth, to be worth.

When we said this book was called *The Book of Knowing and Worth* we are telling you something very important. You must be in your knowing to claim your worth. And without claiming your true worth, your divine heritage, you will not step forward and claim the kingdom, which is your true inheritance.

The passage that you each undergo through the acquisition of this information and through what we will teach you will be one of amazement and fury. And we say amazement, because you will begin to recognize aspects of yourselves that are no longer in alignment, and you will see how silly it was to hold them to you as your true name. And we say fury, because what you will recognize is how you have harmed the self in an attempt to keep yourself small. And once you recognize that is no longer needed, the door opens wide and you step forward into your own manifestation as the Christ in man known to you as you.

Now, each one of you has decided to be a witness to this opportunity for your fellows. When many people read a text at one time, they all go into alignment as a group frequency. And one of the things you will find through the engagement with this text is you will begin to find other people, both in the ethers and on the physical plane, that are attending to these teachings with you. We will encourage this only so you may be in discourse, to be reminded once again that this is a collective action.

We are not doing this just to benefit you, but to be remembered through you each as who and what we are. We are an aspect of the Christ manifested, as are you, so we seek your own remembrance as your true selves so we may be in accord in a wonderful way. The conversations that ensue, we will say, will be more than interesting to you, they will be elevating. And we are making a joke here, yes, but by "elevation" we mean we will lift you as you lift yourselves, and the conversations will do the same.

The group frequency of those attending to this work will have great power. The planet that you are aligned to, this plane of experience you know is at a juncture, is at a reckoning, and the awakening of man is what is required and what is attended to now. We sing your song, each of you, so you may sing the songs yourselves and you may teach the songs to your fellows. And we will ask you this: When you know your words to your own song, to your own expression, why would you not serve your fellows to bring them into alignment with their own divine worth?

Now we are teachers. That is our role here with you. But we know who we are, what we are, and how we serve is how we are expressed. As you each know who and what you are, your expression is manifested as your consciousness and you call to yourselves the circumstances you require to be of service in whatever way is appropriate to you, to you and your gifts, to you and your abilities, to you and your choices.

Your choices are never taken from you, you know. And you must always know this: You always have choice, you always have choice, you always have choice. And as long as you know you have a choice, you are always free. Please know this to be so.

As we will continue with this text, we will be gifting you things, both in frequency and in information, that will align you to a new expression. But the choice to embody, to be manifested as the Christ, will be always yours. The aspect of you that knows this is true already will be doing the work with you, so you are never without aid. And we are here for you as well as we say "Yes" to you each.

Now when we said the chapter of this text was "I Know

Who I Am," we will tell you what that means. "I know who I am" as a manifestation of God in man. I know who I am as a divine creation. I know who I am as the Christ in manifestation. I know who I am as a soul who knows his own song, who sings his own song, who knows her own worth, who expresses her own worth, and on and on and on. As we claim this with you, you align to it now.

We will ask you this: If there were a way to work this text that would be of more benefit to you than we are giving you now, we would require the information from you. As we are your teachers we are also your students, and we understand the limitations that you engage with when you get frightened, when you get confused, when the language is not clear. So we do our very best, yes, as we work through the teacher Paul to teach you. But we ask you this: As you are reading this text, if you require more definition you will ask. You will ask, you will ask, and you will put the thought out to the universe in whatever form you like and it will be attended to by us as this transmission continues.

You understand already that time is a structure and we bypass time. So as we see the text in your hand and we see the confusion or the question, we may attend to it now as the transmission is being delivered.

You understand already that you are the one in choice of your experience with this. We are wondering now if there is a way to put the minds at ease of those who fear this cannot be so. And in that knowing, "I know who I am, I know what I am,

I know how I serve," can there be relief. And we would like to explain this to you now.

You must be in your own worth and be in the claim of your own knowing. There is only one moment you may know in, and that is the present moment. When you claim, "I know who I am, I know what I am, I know how I serve," you are bringing your consciousness into present time in a way that you may feel and be expressed as. You cannot know anything yesterday. You will know nothing tomorrow. You may only know now. When you claim these words, the encoding comes to you and carries your vibration back into present time so that you may know.

If you work with this now, and you work with the claim of truth, "I know who I am, I know what I am, I know how I serve," you will do this with yourselves in a way that you may express. This will temper the worry because it will put you back in the authority to be the one who knows who and what she requires.

Now there is a choice to be made. And the choice that is being made by each of you is to redesign your lives in accordance with your true worth. And your true worth, we say, is the manifestation of God as you. What will this require? What will this be? How will this seem? How will you attend to those things you have known and trusted to be there to support you when they no longer seem relevant or required at this new level of consciousness? How do you trust the new life that you will step into as you move into accord with this teaching? And how do you tell your friends you are now a new woman or a new man? These will be the teachings of this text. They will continue on for the next few months as the dictation is allowed to occur. We are presenting the material as we see fit, and we are already aligned to the requirements of those who will read it.

The manifestation of this text on this plane will be more than significant. It will be a trajectory for many to the infinite possibility of their own soul's expression. And we ask you now if you would like to welcome us in. If you would like to welcome us in, the teachers, the vibration that informs this text you may ask us in now. And there is only one word that is required, and we will teach you this word in our next chapter. And the word is "Welcome." Welcome us, please. Say welcome to us, if you wish, and we are with you.

We will thank you both now for this opportunity to teach and we will say good night. Stop now, please.

TWO

WELCOME

Day Three

Now the work we do today, as we said, is about welcome. And the welcome we call to you, to each one of you, is your own authority, your own mastery, your own requirements for the changes you need to be in your manifestation as your Christed Self. The delivery of this text as it is given to you is a text of authority, and you must claim your authority, each one of you as you read, as you engage, as you decide. If you know that this can be so, and we will underline *know,* you can attend to the teachings very rapidly and welcome them as they come. If you are hesitant about the teachings, you will have to learn to trust yourselves to be the one who can claim their worth as their own teacher as she engages, as he engages, with our language imprinted on this page.

Now we said the title of this chapter was "Welcome," and we will explain welcome. Welcome is an invitation; welcome is an invite to all that can be outside of what you have known. When you decide something can be, you give it power. When you welcome it, you claim it, you call it to you and you allow it. The authority that you have, each and every one of you, to be the one who welcomes your destiny is what we would like to teach you today.

You think small, you know. You think in small ways. "I can grow a little bit today," "I can have my little experience today," and we will say that's okay if you like it. You can have it little all you like. But if you want great change, you must assume great things can be so. And the claim of a great thing, we say, requires you to welcome it in a real way.

When you don't know what you want, you don't do much to get it. You sit around, you wait for things to come, you attend to the things that are presented to you, and that is okay, we will say, in some ways. When you know you want change, when you know you can claim change and stand in your authority and say, "Yes, I welcome change, I call change to me," you must think in a big way and be prepared to receive what can come. What many of you do, you know, is you claim things. You call things to you but you do not accept them, because an aspect of you still believes that you are not allowed, that you cannot hold them, that you are not worthy.

Now the listening we do with you is to hear you when you ask us for guidance, "Can I know myself in a new way?" "Can I attend to myself in a better way than I have?" And of course, we always say yes. Yes, you can. Yes, you are allowed. But you must claim and welcome what you claim. When you welcome something to you, it allows itself to incorporate itself as you, as part of your frequency that can then be brought into manifestation.

We give Paul the image, again and again, of a package being left outside the door. You call something to you, you claim something in your creations that you believe you need, that you require for your growth, and it would like to come. It would like to come to you and be an aspect of your life. But it does not come and you do not know why. We will explain this to you very simply: It has been left outside the front door, in a manner of speaking, and you have not opened the door to receive it, to say "Welcome," to invite it in.

When you can imagine going past a restaurant that you would like to eat in but assume you can never afford the food, you do not enter the restaurant, you do not feel worthy of it. You cannot be in accord with the vibration of what is in there because you have said no, for practical reasons, perhaps. But the other reason, we will say, is you hold a frame that does not allow you to conceive of something new, that would allow you entry to receive what is already there waiting there for you. When you realign yourself, when you realign your ideas of what you can hold, you can welcome that thing to you. You take your seat, you have your meal, you give thanks for what is there, and you do this because you know your worth.

Now the doubt of worth, we say, is claimed by you as well. If you are what you say you are, you are your doubts and fears as you decide them. If you wish to relinquish them, you have the opportunity to do so here. The requirements for this are very simple. Change your mind. Change your mind. Change your mind and decide that you can have what you say that you need. Open the door and say, "Welcome." Say welcome to what can be, what you may allow, what you may be in accord with in a new way.

Now we will decide something for you, and we will do this with your permission. You are allowed to change. Underline this, please: *You are allowed to change.* Who would tell you you could not? Who would have that authority over you to say you cannot be who you are in the truest way available to you? The aspect of you that we will say is the Christ seeks her expression, seeks his expression, and will do so as she gives herself permission to realign every aspect of her life to that knowing that this can be so. We welcome you now to what will be, to what can be, as you say yes.

Now we have some things to discuss with you about what you say you want. And we have discussed this before and we will discuss it again. Much of what you claim you do so out of an obligation to what you were taught. "I should have the house on the hill," "I should have the job with the title," so you concur with the paradigm of the "should" and you run about your business creating these things for yourselves as if they are actually important.

If we show Paul a board game of Monopoly with the pieces laid out and the dice rolling and the piles of money being taken away and the houses being built and restored and the board game being thrown off the table, you will see how silly this all really is. It's a game that you adhere to, that you agree to play with your fellows. The only rules that are created, you know, are the ones that you attend to, are the ones that you decide together and if you wish to change them, you may. But as long as you are in your obligation to your history, "It must be so because I was taught it was," you will be in deceit about your true nature and what you may hold as your true self.

We are not saying there is anything wrong with a job title as long as you understand that the title that you have can be taken from you, means very little in the scheme of things, is an emblem that you wear to show others your achievement, or to give them the convenience of knowing who you are in your role. The true nature of yourself has no job title, is a manifestation of the Creator, and would like only to align more and more to what she can be as she expresses this.

We have talked about dominion before and dominion being what you can claim. "I know who I am, I know what I am, I know how I serve," is such a claim. But the dominion that you hold, all of you collectively, is this plane of existence that you work through in order to be expressed in your true nature.

How you align in your worth does not adhere to historical paradigms of achievement, and you must understand this, please: The historical emblemization of wealth, of prosperity, of success was created in a way to create a system of governance. The rich have what they get, the poor need what the rich have, and so on and so on and so on. Once you begin to understand that each and every being here has the right to the kingdom, to the inheritance of All That Is, you begin a remarkable transformation; you no longer acquire things as a way to prove your worth. You are instilled in your own worth, your life reflects your own worth and, consequently, you can attend to the worth of your fellows.

When you attend to the worth of your fellows, you do something very simple: You know who they are. You know who they are in truth. You know what they are in this manifestation and you know how they serve at this level of consciousness that they are attending to. Now we give you this not only as an example, but as a way of knowing something in your consciousness. We do not give you these words to parrot, to recite, we give you these words to claim, to claim, to claim. When you claim something, you call it into being. You say welcome to the new possibilities that are inherent in the claim, and the claim brings to you the transformation that you require. When you claim to a fellow, "I know who you are, I know what you are, I know how you serve," you are not just recognizing something, you are instilling in them energetically the creation that we work with in this text.

The language that we work with with you has been encoded to impress upon each energy field a system of transformation that will align you to your Christed Self. Now, this must be done in intent, yes, but you can witness the Christ in a fellow, "I know who you are," and decide for them that this is their truth. You don't do this over the objections of anybody, you do not do this in opposition of anything, you are simply witnessing and claiming what is eternally so.

When you decide that the worth of another is the incarnation of the Christ in manifestation before you regardless of what they think, what they have been taught, or how they act, you begin to align to a level of consciousness that will supersede all judgment and lift you in a vision to the Christ in manifestation as man. "Ye are all sons of God." That has been said, and it is true. But you cannot know this and not go about it. It must be demonstrated by you in your actions and in the visions you hold of your fellows.

The big difference in this text with what we have taught you previously is that we are moving you beyond conjecture and beyond energetic vibration to physical manifestation, embodiment, and expression of yourself in the highest way you can hold. If you wish to hold this, you must make some decisions for yourself.

1. I am worthy of this.
2. She, he, everybody, everybody is worthy of this, and
3. Nothing can be so that I do not claim in my worth.

Now we will explain what we just said: You must know that you can be this thing. As you do this, you must know that everybody can hold this frequency and then you must take responsibility for the fact that everything in your frequency is projecting outward and claiming the things that you hold in your vibration manifested in physical form. The alignment to this truth obligates you in a beneficial way to know that you can change.

You have been given the authority, you do not know how to use it, and we are teaching you today.

You all hold vibration. You are always in frequency. You are always calling to you the things you require to know yourselves through. You know this much because we have taught you. Others have said similar things. What we teach you today is the requirement for alignment to the Christ consciousness embodied as you, which you must welcome and claim for yourself, in your fellows, and know that it can be so.

We are choosing to do this with you in our authority to support mankind in elevating herself, himself, itself, if you wish, to the next level of incarnation that can be absorbed by the species, by each of you as you relinquish the old paradigm that was born in separation and was born in fear.

You are each lifting, you know. Everybody on the planet right now is in process of acclimating to the vibration of the Christ that is here, is here, is here. But many of you don't know what is going on. You go into turmoil. You take the responsibility to create that has been gifted to you and you use it in ways that are not healthy because you don't know what else to do.

You each live your lives, you know, through a system of expression. You wake up in the morning; you are expressed with what you do through your choices and your actions. Your expression, we say, is always a reflection of the consciousness you hold. Your consciousness, we say, is born in what you know, and what you hold, and what you believe. As you shift out of a paradigm of limitation, you require yourselves to grow up as a spiritual being and the grown-up, we say, takes responsibility for all of her creations. And we say, first and foremost, the creation that you must attend to is how you treat yourself and all of your fellows.

When you deny the Christ in your fellows, you deny the Christ in yourself. You pull the shade down over the window, you obscure the light and you walk in darkness. Now how do you release what holds you, what binds you in your dark room? You decide something else. The decision, we say, to be in transformation will align you to transformation. As we have taught you, what you judge you fear, and who you judge is who you are afraid of. If what you witness before you, regardless of what you think, is a manifestation of God, who are you to judge?

Now Paul is asking, "But what if they did something horrible, don't I get to judge that?" Absolutely not. No one has given you the authority to judge your fellows. If you wish to claim it, you may, but what you incur is your own separation. As you incur separation from your fellows, you have decided that you are separate from your Creator. There can be no other way.

Now, there is a discipline at hand here and we will have to attend to that. You are not used to this. You are not worthy, in your own minds, of being forgiven, so how can you forgive your fellows? This is what you've been brought up with, you know. This is what you have believed, and this is what you create through.

We will give you an opportunity right now, if you like, to create a new way of being:

"I know who I am in my choice to be. I know what I am in my choice to be. I know how I serve in my choice to be."

Now we will tell you what this means: You are always choosing.

"I am choosing to be forgiven. I am choosing to align myself to the forgiveness of myself for anything and everything I may have thought, done, said, believed, any justice I believe must be brought to me from anything I may have ever done in any time. I now align myself to my own freedom as the one who has the authority to say I have permission to be released from my own unforgiveness of myself."

Now we will tell you what you just did. You just decided something. You decided that you can change something. Once you make the decision, you can claim it; once you claim it, you must welcome it; and as you welcome it, it moves into accord as your energy field and it aligns as you. When you forgive yourself, when you can see yourself as being worthy of forgiving, you know you can forgive your fellows. When you can forgive your fellows, you are free, you are free, you are free.

This has always been so. But you live in a society where you believe that those who were judged, who were penalized, were worthy of judgment. Now, we are not talking about actions against man that would incur a response. We are telling you something very different. What you hold in your consciousness as unforgiveness of your fellows you call to yourself again and again and again.

If somebody takes the bread from the store, you may decide that something must happen to someone who steals the bread, but you do not judge the man. The act is what is being attended to. The act of the man and the man are two different things. The act of the man is always reflective of his consciousness, whatever the act may be, because man can only attend to himself at the level of consciousness that he can hold. But do you forgive the man? Yes. And if the man needs bread, feed the man, don't put him in jail.

When you understand that you are your brother's keeper, each and every one of you, and the way to attend to your brother is to witness him in his worth, you align to your Christed Self and you transform your life. Your life, we say, as you have lived it, has been the product of all your beliefs, and the changes that will come to you as you align to this level of consciousness and manifest it as yourself will show you who you always were: "I know who I am, what I am, how I serve."

Now this, as we said, is an encoding of language that carries with it a vibrational power. When you work with this decree, you will feel the frequency of it. It will call you to it. It will call you back into present time, which is the only time you may know anything. When you are frightened of yourself, when you are in a situation you do not know what to do with, you may use these words to anchor yourself back into your vibration as your true self. You will feel the shift in vibration as you come home to your true self.

When you attend to your brothers in the same way, "I know who you are, what you are, how you serve," you align their vibration to their own worth and to their own knowing, and you support them in shifting out of a paradigm of lack, of fear, of knowing not what they are but what they have been. Now the joy that you bring to your fellows as you lift them is what is sung by you as your consciousness.

We want to discuss something with Paul for a moment, who is getting in the way today. He does not like the channeling. He wants other information that he has known, that will make him feel secure in this teaching. As Paul is a student of this text, he must learn as well, and we would like to continue our lecture without his interruption. As Paul interrupts we have to decide whether or not to attend to his interruptions and we decide not to. The work that we are doing with the students of this text will be here much longer after Paul is, and Paul must understand that his job here is to be the receiver, and the language that comes through him is not his responsibility.

Now we want to discuss something new, which is blame. And we want to talk about blame for a minute as a structure. When you blame somebody else, for anything and everything, you decide that you are a victim. When you claim yourself as a victim, you incur victimhood and your life reflects this in all ways.

Many of you get in difficulties when you have had situations in your life that you believe could not be forgiven. "He left me for that woman." "He killed this person." "He took these things I own." And while these things happen to you, you are the one who must claim how you are in response to them. If you elect to stay in a place of blame, you continue to tether yourself to the person you want to blame and to bind yourself to your history. And the very history you would like to let go of to move on with your life, that you condemn, is what you tie yourself to as the one who blames.

So how do you move beyond blame? How do you learn a new way of being? How do you decide something different in a new way when what you have known, when what you have been taught, is to blame somebody else for what occurs in your life? You decide that you can. "I know who I am, what I am, how I serve" will bring you, once again, into alignment with your true nature. When you know who you are, you know that you are the one accountable to all of your choices, and that includes how you respond to anything and everything that has occurred historically that you would decide has created your problems.

Once you realize that you are the prisoner of your own rage, of your own condemnation to all of your fellows, you will begin to liberate yourself. But you must know that self-identification will be the key to your freedom. If you know that you are the one who is allowed to forgive, who is able to forgive, who is able to transform her history through a new idea, and you will say, "I can be free," you will lift your consciousness above the wall that has created the separation that you exist in.

We like this metaphor and we will use it again. Imagine that you are standing facing a wall. You cannot see your way through it. On the other side of the wall is all that might be, all that might be gifted to you, but you do not see the way through it. If you would like to take a hammer and bang on the wall, you may be banging for a very long time.

Your vibration, we say, which is sound and concentrated energy, has the power to displace any wall, any obstacle that you may have known. If you can imagine yourself growing greater in your being and taller in your frequency, you will see over the wall that you have created to what has always been on the other side. And what is on the other side of the wall, we will say, is you in your freedom as the one who knows who she is.

The alignment to the Christ as you is an event. We would underline this: *The alignment to the Christ as you is an event.* It is a thing that happens. It is not something that is decided upon and then nothing happens. It is decided upon by you, in manifestation, in accordance with your worth and as you claim it, your entire energy field must be realigned to the new authority, to the new authority you have gifted yourself with.

Now, the aspect of you that gets authority is not the personality. Not the one who wants peas for dinner and likes a walk in the park on Saturdays. It is the aspect of you that is eternal, that can be re-created through and as you in this manifestation. Some of you believe that if you do this, you will disappear. And we would admonish you, those who want to disappear have an issue to take up with yourself. Abnegating the self on any level is never the work of this text. The work of this text is aligning the aspect of you that is true to receive itself in primacy over those aspects of the self that were used to running herd over all areas of your life, that were accepting history as fact and not illusion.

Now we will tell you that history is an illusion in one way, because you remember your history, and you remember your history as it was reported to you, or as it was framed by you. And a frame, we will say, is the structure that you hold before you that you see the world through. If you would imagine that you are holding a little window before your face with just enough room for your eyes to peer out, you would see how you operate in limitation. The frame that you hold is the one that you have accepted. It is how you see yourself, what you have known, and how you attend to your world today.

As we will discuss framing in a later chapter, we will not go into detail now. But we would like you to know that the history you claim is born out of your perceptions, and your perceptions have been limited because you thought you were your body, you thought you were what happened to you, you thought you were who you were told you were by science, by the priest or the rabbi, and you believed it all because you were not told anything different.

Moving into manifestation as the one who knows who she is, who he is, is a great adventure. And what happens on an adventure, as you know, is you confront things that may be challenging, that may not be expected, that may be brought to you to overcome to see what you are made of. If you do not test yourself, which simply means, if you do not engage the practice we offer you in a way that challenges what you have known, you will not realize the truth of the work that we are giving to you, nor will you know what you are capable of as the one who can surmount the illusion of her history.

"The illusion of your history." What an amazing way to think of something. If you would, right now, take a moment and think of your entire history up until now. Everything you have been through, known yourself through, decided from, and imagine, for a moment, that it is an illusion. That it was never really there. They were things, they were occurrences that were brought through, you have your memory of them. But the memory that you hold is all informed by things that you were taught and ways to recognize things.

We are teaching Paul this at this time as well. He is seeing in his mind's eye the image of a jack-o'-lantern and he is saying, "That is a jack-o'-lantern." It is only a jack-o'-lantern because that is what somebody once said it was. It is a pumpkin that has been carved that illumines itself with a candle inside. It has been transformed by a new name. What you think of something and how you claim something and how you know what you have been and where you have been is shared information and recognition of what you were all taught.

Now we will tell you what illusion is. Illusion is Maya. Illusion is the material world that you live in that you give so much credence to. When you give credence to everything in physical form as being finite, you lose sight of the infinite. And when you move past the finite to the infinite, you begin to move beyond the illusion of your history and you understand physical reality simply to be a manifestation of consciousness that you are all sharing and agreeing to.

The lives that you have lived up until now were created by you to bring you to this juncture, where you will know yourself in a new way. We ask you this: Who in this reading would like to know herself, would like to know himself as an aspect of the Creator? If you would like to do this with us now, we would like to align you to our vibration through the act of welcome. If you would sit for a moment and be still in your body and feel the energy field that you hold around you, if you would do this with us, we would like to gift you with an experience of welcome.

We would like you now to align every cell in your being, every conscious receiver in your being that you have, to align to the frequency of welcome. We are inviting you right now to say welcome with every aspect of you. And what are you welcoming, you may ask? You are welcoming that aspect of you that is the Creator in manifestation. You will say this with us now if you would:

I am Word through my body, Word I am Word.
I am Word through my vibration, Word I am Word.
I am Word through my knowing of myself as Word.

And in this moment we invite you to welcome us, your teachers, the Christ consciousness, all the aspects of you that are seeking to be brought into manifestation in alignment with your true self. And we would like you to say yes. Say yes, now if you would, and welcome us as you, as the aspect of you that you are aligning to.

We are all of the same stuff, you know. We are all of Christ consciousness. We are simply in different levels of our awareness of this. As you move into consciousness, you realign all things, you co-resonate with all things in a new way. And our vibration, as we would teach you, is here to shepherd you. You may align to us at any moment simply by saying, "Welcome." If you wish to practice it now, you may. In your mind, say the word "welcome" and allow our frequency to be in attendance to you in a way that you may know.

Now we are authorized to do this by you as you allow it and align to it. We take nothing from you, and what we do with you is support you in your own achievement as the one who chooses herself to be on this journey to her own recognition, to his own recognition of his divine worth. You are aligned now to the extent that you are allowed to.

Now, what does it mean, "to the extent that you are allowed to"? We take you through a process here of alignment and removal of obstacles and obstructions that you have created or inherited in order to know yourself through limitation. As we attend to these, you lift your vibration to the extent that you allow yourself to lift, and we shift you as you allow us to shift you. Now we work with you each, the readers of this text, in frequency to support this, but you must say "welcome."

Now we will explain what we did when we asked you to

claim, "I am Word." If you are new to our teaching, you may not know that the frequency we attend to we claim as the Word, which is the energy of the Creator in action. The aspect of you that is already this is awakened through this choice to self-identify as the frequency.

When you claim, "I am Word through my body," you bring the physical being that you are in accordance to that frequency of the Word. When you claim "I am Word through my vibration," you align your energy field to the frequency of the Word. When you claim, "I am Word through my knowing of myself as Word," you realign your true self, the identity that you hold, in recognition of your worth as the aspect of the Creator that can be realized in form. And our definition of the Christ, and the one that we offer here, is that the Christ is the aspect of the Creator that can be realized in material form as you.

Now we thank you each for your attendance today. And we would like to resume very quickly with the continuation of this chapter. We would like to make a date with Paul and Victoria to resume next week. We have much to teach and we are encouraging you to make yourselves available for the sessions as they are needed.

We understand that you have obligations in the world, but the teaching that we are giving you now bears great significance and the times are coming very quickly that mankind will need to attend to himself through the information that we gift you with. So we would say yes to you, we will support you in making this possible in any way that we can.

We say yes to you as you say yes to yourselves. And we say to each of you, "Welcome." Stop now, please.

Day Four

How come you don't know who you are? How come you deny yourself your abilities? How come you cannot believe that the love of God would hold you in any situation you could encounter? How come you do not know you are free? How come you do not care that you are imprisoned by structure, by belief, by history? Because you said, "I am willing to give my authority to whoever will take it. I am willing to let my life be dictated by whatever thing would claim dominion over my life."

These are the thoughts you hold, you know, when you render yourself powerless in the face of situations. "Why did I create this?" you may ask yourself. "Why did I choose this?" You always choose in accordance with your beliefs, and your beliefs are what you know and what you have held to be true.

Now, to counter these things that you have created, you must come into a new way of being, a new ideal, if you wish, of what can be. And the welcome we offered yesterday to our dominion, to work with us in concurrence with your own needs, will sing you a new song, and a song in praise of the Creator who makes all things new.

Now when you ask for something in spirit and you expect it to appear in the material, you must know that the issue that you ask for must be in agreement with your soul's worth. There is nothing that you can create on this material plane that you could bring into recognition in material form that is not in congruence with what you believe you are worth. You cannot create the kingdom of heaven here when you do not believe you are worthy of it.

Now, the kingdom of God, we would say, is the manifestation of God as you, as out-pictured through you, through each of you, in your beneficence, in your kindness, in your love, in your willingness to serve. But the frightening thing about this for all of you is that you do not want it. You believe that it is a negative, that you will lose your self-worth that you have attained through structures that have been erected to give you an appearance of dominion when you, in fact, have been enslaved by them.

When you are enslaved by a structure that you have created, you are the only worker in the factory that stays alight twenty-four hours seeking to replicate what it has created again and again and again. The structure will fall away, we say, and the true worker inside the factory, the one who has been given to create, will realize himself as an aspect of the whole, and the next creation he can attend to is the creation of God in man out-pictured in all things that would be welcomed by you each.

If you say you cannot have something, you cannot have it. If you believe it can be so, you move into a new creation, a new possibility. If you align to the new possibility, the new possibility is gone into congruence with you in material form, and it will be manifested. When you understand this, that your worth is the key and that what you would claim is always in accordance with your worth, you begin to think outside of yourself. And you begin to think of the larger issues that present you each as a species, as a civilization, as an aspect of the Creator operating in tandem with others.

The belief that you are alone and insignificant is a key thing here. If you know you are not alone and if you know you have significance, what you attend to changes. The disempowerment you have experienced so far on this plane to mechanize yourself in accordance with existing structures has attended to your fear, to your misplacement of your true identity. But the coming days of this text, we will say, will be to walk you forward with our hand in yours attending to yourself as one who may be worthy of the kingdom. "The Kingdom," we say, will be the title of a future chapter, but you must understand already that that is where this road is taking you.

Paul has a memory from his childhood, where his hand was held by his father's, and he was taken on a journey through a system where the world of the future was portrayed before him.[2] He looked at the world before him in wonder and saw what could be in another time, and those things became real to him because somebody else took the time to create them, to show him what may be so. In some ways we are doing this with the readers of this book. We are taking you each by hand to welcome you to what can be as yourselves as you coexist as a

---

2 What is being referenced is an exhibit at the 1965 New York World's Fair.

species, as a civilization, who honors the truth of who each of
you are.

Will this happen in this lifetime? Yes. This is the lifetime
where it *can* happen, as enough of you attend to your worth, to
your divinity, and the divinity in all things. The kingdom, we
say, is the anchoring of the frequency of the Christ consciousness on this plane of existence. The trials that mankind has
faced, without exception, have been the trials that have been
born in separation. When you realize you are no longer separate from your true selves, or from the true selves of your fellows, you begin to listen differently and the music that is
playing will be heard, will be heard, will be heard.

Now the jurisdiction you have, each and every one of you, as
a manifestation of the Creator in form, is far greater than you
believe. You did not know that you can change your lives in
significant ways because you were told that there were systems
to work through that you must attend to. "Before you can go to
tenth grade, you have to go to first." "Before you can go to tenth
grade, you have to learn the lessons." And the lessons are se-
quenced in such a way to give you a procedural way of learning.
Now, this is not wrong-minded when you realize from first to
tenth is a long expanse of time. You can also understand that
how you direct your frequency now will shift you in a way that
the lessons may come as you are ready. And you can take two
classes at a time, you know. You can learn many things at once.

How you attend to your learning, how you welcome your
learning, if you wish, is up to you. You are the one in charge

here. Our hands are being open toward you in welcome to shepherd you through to the walk, to the path, to the idea, to whatever you need to respond to yourselves in your worth, in your worth, in your worth.

Now, when you have a fear of your own journey, the tendency is to unpack your bag and sit on your couch and say, "Well, I will receive a postcard from somebody else. If they say that this is a good journey, maybe I will take it." You have to decide for yourselves what your adventure can be. How you attend to yourself as the one on the adventure will of course be your choice, but we are giving you usherance to bring you forward and to say yes to you to walk your own path.

The significance of the path that you walk on is that it is your own. The way to the glory of the Creator has been designed by you at a soul level, and the path that you will walk to get there, with or without our instruction, will be known by you only through your own experience. And we must underline this, yes, *only through your own experience.* Secondhand knowledge of the divine makes for a pretty painting on the wall of a church, but it does not give you the knowing you need to attend to yourself as the one who walks her own path, has her own witness, shares her own name with others, "I know who I am, what I am, how I serve," and finds the key to the kingdom on the palm of her own hand.

The gates that you walk through when you attend to this path are the prisons that you have held yourself through, in abeyance with, in creations that you have created with the agreement of your fellows. As each door is opened, the path widens. As the path widens, you encounter your fellows who are your journeyers, your fellow journeyers, and you have companions on the road in song, in song, in song.

Now, the shepherds that we are, we will say, are not new. We have been here for a very long time, and we have been attending to you each in preparation for your journey. We know who you are already, you know, those who come to the glory of the kingdom, and your names are known by us in light, in light, in light.

Your names, we say, are not the ones you have been gifted with in this lifetime, but they are the ones that are known by us as you. Yes, in fact, we do know who you are, what you are, and how you serve. And the kingdom is for you to be remembered through. We will tell you who we are in one way or another as we continue with this text, but for this moment we think of you as our students and our teachers. And as we progress, we will tell you new things to instill in you the knowing that you need to create yourselves in your new possibilities.

Now the trajectory you have chosen and continue to choose as you read is one of wonder.

"May I be in my wonder in every day. May I allow myself to be in wonder in every choice I make."

As you claim this for yourself, you claim yourself, you open to new possibilities. The windows begin to open and what was stale releases. The new air comes in and fills the room with new choice, new ability, new love. The ideas that we give you to sort through, to choose from, to decide with, will be there for you as you need them.

The trajectory we are choosing, you say, is one of wonder. Attending to yourself in wonder, as the one who may be in the new trajectory, is what we ask for you today. "Am I willing to claim myself as the one who may be in wonder? Am I willing to align myself to the possibilities that come to me as I align myself to wonder? Will I listen to myself, to the new thoughts that are gifted to me with each choice that I make, with each idea that comes, with each belief I hold, so that I may know something new?"

We ask you this: When you know what you know, must you act on it? And we will tell you, yes. When you have new knowledge—and new knowledge, we say, is new information that you have gone into agreement with *in your knowing*—it becomes part of your frequency and the reckoning with it is nearly instantaneous. To reckon with something is to face it, to see it for what it is, and then to move with it as you choose.

As you decide something new, as the claim of truth is gifted to you and you move into a new idea, and we say to you "idea" as possibility, and you move into your knowing in this issue, you may claim it, it becomes you, and your life reflects it immediately.

Now when you ask yourself a question and you deny yourself the answer because you do not want to hear it, you create a problem of mistrust of the self and mistrust of the information that you are being gifted with. So we would encourage each of you to begin to record your answers as you go into inquiry with yourselves. "What do I want for myself?" "What do I no longer need?" "What have I cared too much for?" "What have I cared too little for?" "What have I agreed to that is no longer true, and what would a new belief be that would liberate from me the things I have attended to as myself that cannot truly be myself because I now know who I am in my wonder?"

When you work with a record, you have an ability to remember, to see, and to decide anew. But many of you are so unconscious about your actions—and to be unconscious in an action means that you must have been unconscious in the intent behind the action—that the record will give you responsibility to decide, to decide, to decide when you know something.

Now when you know something, "I am in my knowing," you are in resonance with something. It is not an idea, it is not an intellectual structure, it is a way of being. Knowing and being happen simultaneously. You cannot know and not be at the same time. You are this thing that you know because you are in agreement with it. You can agree with an idea, but you are not an idea. You can agree with what's for dinner, but you are not what's for dinner. When you know something in your being, you are in tandem with it, you are in resonance as it, and it is created through you. "I know who I am" is such a claim. And as we welcome you to this claim in a true way, we must align the energy field that you know yourself through to be in agreement with it. As we have said welcome to you and asked you to invite your energy field, all that was receptive in you, to welcome us, we are taking you in the journey to receptivity. And to be in receipt is to be in allowance, and to be in allowance is to be in welcome.

The creations that you know yourself through, each and every one of you, that you have agreed upon, chosen, decided would be there because they must be there, will begin to be altered as you go into agreement with the new knowing that you have. What you believe to be so solid, in fact, is not so solid and is instead a creation born in your system that has been out-pictured by you to perceive. Now, when you decide something new, your landscape must be altered to reflect the new knowing, and this will be seen by each of you as your journey forward with us.

The path that you are walking has been trod by many before you, but they believe themselves to be special, or you were told that this was the path of the priest, or the Benedictine, or the sage. You were not told that the path that you are walking is the path of your own soul's worth. And the only things that you divest yourself of on this path are the things that you no longer require to know yourself through. You may still have a nice house, you know, and be on your path. You may still be in love and enjoy the world around you. When we speak of sacrifice, we simply mean investment. And what you sacrifice is your attachment to who and what you thought you were. And those creations that you have used to decide these things must be altered as you begin to know yourselves anew.

Now we welcome you each to the pathway. We would like you to imagine in your mind's eye that you are standing before a gate. It is a wooden gate. It has been there a very long time. As you stand before the gate, you acknowledge your life as you stand there, as you witness the gate, as you ponder what might be before you. And we will open the gate for you now, and we will take you by the hand and we will begin to lead you. The only thing that we ask is that you allow yourself to trust that you are being led well. That your highest interests are always in mind. That there is no need to deceive and that there is only love in the action we offer you.

The path that we are leading you on is the path of your own soul. And your own soul, we say, is what you are incarnating as in the highest way available to you. As you begin to walk down this path, you learn new lessons, you have encounters, and you are witnessed by us, by your fellows. And as the landscape changes, all change comes to you in accordance with the vibration that you hold, so you may laugh, you may run, you may sing, you may choose your own way as the decider of your fate.

As we walk you forward, know that your freedom is at the end of this. And the freedom from bondage we say, always, always, always is the freedom from fear. As we are liberating you individually, we are shifting the structure on this plane that you coexist in. As one man realizes himself without fear, he gives permission for the multitude to do the same. When you are in co-resonance with that man, your freedom is inherent in the choice to stand before yourself in the acknowledgment that this can be so. Each one of you gives permission to your fellows, you know.

As one man realizes the gifts of the kingdom, he gives permission to his fellows to do the same. This is not done through proselytizing. This is not even done through language. This is your energy field in its perfect, liberated state, anointing the energy fields of others through recognition of who and what they truly are as well.

As we explained to you earlier, "I know who you are, I know what you are, I know how you serve" is a claim of truth you give your fellows, and the anointing that you give them through this is the welcome they need to find their own garden gate, to swing it open, and to begin their own journey forth.

We said the chapter would be called "Welcome." And now we will say we will end this chapter with this praise:

As we sing the songs of our readers, as we remember them by name, we anoint them to their own possibility that they may be listened to, heard, and healed. As we sing your song for you, we sing your possibilities. And we see you each as rising to them, as hearing yourself in perfect song. We sing your song in wonder, we sing your song in welcome, and we will talk to you soon.

Thank you each and good night. Stop now, please.

THREE

RESPONSIBILITY

Day Five

We're ready to speak about responsibility and your desires, and why you must hold yourself accountable for all things you choose. You understand that when you choose something, you go into a relationship with it. It is your decision. And what you have chosen, you claim. And as you claim it, you become accountable to it. Everything you have ever claimed, born in whatever reasons were there when you claimed it, you have responsibility for.

Now this is not to frighten you. It's about giving you freedom. When you have responsibility for something, you have a choice to deal with it in one way or another. You can be accountable to it in whatever way you believe. But what we would like to tell you now is that your choice to be responsible to yourself as the one in authority, who claims herself as worthy of what she says she wants, will create a new life for you. And what you claim will always call you forward.

Now we want to address something before this tape goes further. We are trying to speak through Paul, who has resistance today. So we would like to begin again. And we are going to say, "Begin again," to move him out of the way so this recording may happen as it is required to. Now, Paul, we want you to do one thing before we go any further: Step aside, step aside, step aside and let us come forward as we may, as we may sing our song through you. Now we will begin again:

We speak of responsibility today. Everything you have chosen you are accountable to. Understand this, everybody. When you make a claim, when you make a decision, you call something to you and you are in relationship with that thing you have claimed and consequently you are responsible to it. As you accelerate in vibration, what you call to yourself changes. You align to new possibilities. New things may be born and inherited by you in your own knowing of what you can be accountable to.

Now the fear that you have of this, and has always been, is one of responsibility. "Can I afford to be responsible for my creations when I don't know what I am doing, when I am claiming in my history, when I am doing what I have been told?" We will tell you this: Everything you have chosen, you have chosen for a reason. As your reasons for choosing change, you will align to a new knowing and your choices will be in accord with new worth.

Now we want to tell you one thing before we go any further: This is not about regret. We are not teaching you that you have to sift through every choice you have ever made and look at where you were accountable. You are accountable, you know, because your life is reflecting the choices you have made. Do you understand this? The evidence is everything you know and perceive. You agree to these things because they are on the horizon. You witness them every day. They are the lives that you lead.

Nothing will change without permission on a higher level by you to attend to your own soul's worth. Until you do this in fullness, you continue to operate in worry, in fear, in choices that were made in obligation and not in the true knowing of your worth.

Now we want to teach you today about what you are responsible to: Everything. Everything. Everything. And we would like you to understand this. *You are responsible to everything that you claim.* "I claim I am unhappy," claims you as the one responsible for that choice. "I claim myself in my worth" makes you responsible as the one who claims his worth. What you are not accountable to is not in your purview, you have not agreed to, you have not chosen. But if you can imagine right now that everything you see before you you have agreed to because it could not be there without permission, you will understand the volume that your responsibility extends to.

Now look at this in one way, if you would. When you are responsible to something, you have choices to make. You have a plant. Do you want to water it or not? How do you attend to these things that you have claimed and agreed to? We would like to tell you one thing: You agree to things in a way that you have ascribed to without thought. And the first thing we need you to do to become accountable is to wake up to who and what you are so you may realize once and for all that how you are choosing, why you are choosing, is a product of fear and claims of low self-esteem and low worth.

Your negation of your power as the one who can claim the kingdom is what is being addressed today so you may, once and for all, decide you are free of it. Do you create the sunset? Yes. Because your perception of the sunset has given it its form, its name, its experience in your field. Do you claim your relationships? Yes. Are you in authority over your relationships? Yes. Are you in control of them? No. And we want you to understand something different: You do not control the sunset but you have authority as the one who perceives. You do not control your relationships but you have chosen them in congruence with your beliefs and, consequently, you have authority over them.

Now, authority and control are two different things. When you have authority, you know who you are in relationship to something. When you are in control, you are the decider of it. You are not always the decider, you know, but you are always in choice about how you attend to your creations.

Now, if you are in a relationship and your partner abandons you for whatever reasons, you may feel like a victim but you also have choice. And the ability to know that you have choice— that you can relate to a situation in one way or another—claims you in your authority. You are not passive to experience when you choose to accept something. You go into accord with what is presented to you so you may choose something differently when you are ready. The belief that you are in control of the person who leaves you is a falsehood, but you are always in authority about what you choose to know and agree with.

Now if we want to make a distinction for you, we will attend to that as we may. When you decide something, you are claiming something. When you decide something, you choose it. When somebody leaves you, you did not choose that. But you have the authority and the claim to transform a relationship to a situation in regard to your worth.

Now understand this, please: When you know who you are, what you are, how you serve, your life must move into accord with this. This is a statement of truth. It does not preclude people doing things that you say you do not want. It does not change things that have been manifested by you in lower consciousness. It allows you to transform these things in awareness of your new frequency. "I know who I am" always, always, always is a claim of truth.

Now as your life is transformed in choice, as what you have gone into agreement with changes, what you are responsible to is transformed. Now we will ask you this: What is one thing in your life that you would change if you could? What is one thing you would claim if you were allowed, if you believed it could be? What is one choice you would make anew if you believed there was a possibility that it could be in manifestation? As you choose this thing now, as you decide the new possibility and claim your worth, "I know who I am, I know what I am, I know how I serve," you align to the new possibility that may be created in your authority. If you decide right now that this one thing that you ask for that may be transformed is allowed to be transformed, you can look at a new choice.

Now we want to ask you something. What would happen to your lives if you truly knew that you were the one in authority? We will tell you one thing: You could not blame anybody anymore. You could no longer be a prisoner to your history because you understand that your history was created at a level of consciousness that you are not now in accordance with.

You understand now that every choice you make is in congruence with your new worth and, consequently, claimed by you in your authority. How you attend to these choices that you make in your lives, in your choices, as the one who knows who she is, is what we are speaking to now. The responsibility of your choice to be here now, absorbing this text, aligning to the information we give you, is what you are choosing in this moment. If you know now that every moment of the day you are in choice and, consequently, in authority, you will understand very quickly how strong you are.

The belief that you are not allowed this, that you are not allowed to land in a terrain where you are the authority, where you have choices that can be realized, is what has been withheld from you, and it what is being offered to you anew at this juncture.

The planet that you live on is in a time of transformation. And the transformation, as we see it, is man in relation to her own identity as the aspect of the Creator manifested in form. As you attend to this truth, you become accountable to it as the creator of your world. The belief that you hold, that each of you hold, that this must not be so is where you get caught. It is the trip wire you fall over again and again as you scramble for freedom. "But I cannot go out the door. Out the door is something I don't know. If I go out the door, I will not know who I am." Now, we have told you who you are, again and again, and we will continue to as you allow us to. But you need the experience of yourselves as the one in choice to know that this is so.

When you asked yourself earlier what was the one thing you would change if you could, you must ask now of yourself why it is not changed, why you do not align to the new choice. "Why don't I leave the marriage?" "Why don't I give up the job?" "Why don't I change paths?" "Why don't I give myself the freedom I know I can have?" The truth of this, we say, has always been the inhibition of the Divine Self as withheld by the personality who has gone into an agreement with a paradigm of control.

We want to open this for you now. In this moment we would like you to imagine that you are standing in the middle of a circle. A circle, a circle, a circle that surrounds you. And on the perimeters of this circle, on the outside perimeter, we would like you to list in your mind's eye all of those things that you would claim for yourselves that you perceive to be out of reach.

"The partner I would love to be with," "The awareness of my worth that I can't seem to hold," "The freedom of judgment of myself and my fellows," "The abundance I need to live well and to trust that my worth is not contained by an outside authority." Whatever you would claim for yourself, imagine it on the perimeter of that circle, just outside that line you have drawn in your mind.

Now if you understand right now that everything you have written or decided was on the perimeter of the circle is something that you don't have, you will see that you are already keeping you from yourself. It is not in agreement with you because it is outside of the circle; it is outside what you have claimed for yourself. But now it is new, it is recorded in your mind's eye or, if you wish, on a piece of paper as something that is now a possibility that lives just outside the gate of your soul. Do you understand this? The thing that you once thought could not be, is existing outside of the line that you have created, and just beyond it.

Now what we would like you to do once again is see yourself in the center of the circle. And imagine that around the circle is the line that you have drawn, the perimeter, the border that keeps all things from you. And we want you to extend the circle to include all those things you wrote. So what was outside of the perimeter is now included in it, within the circle you have drawn.

What you are doing right now is making a decision that those things that exist beyond the self can be inherited as you, in your field, and as you express them as in your field, you can call them into manifestation. Every time you think of something as a possibility, you create a new offering for your soul to express itself in a new way.

Every possibility that you can imagine, if you were to imagine it floating around you like a bird, if you can imagine these things landing in your palms and being called to your heart, you would understand what we are telling you. When a possibility is claimed by you, you can hold it. As you hold it, you have gone into agreement with it and it can go into manifestation on this plane.

As you know yourself as the creator of your world and you understand that you have responsibility to yourselves, you will understand that this responsibility extends around you, not only to your own creations but those creations that are shared by all men. You all share the same landscape. You all drink from the same well. If the water is poisoned in the well, none of you will benefit. So you must decide today that what you are doing on your own behalf you are also doing in attendance to the needs of your fellows.

The frightening thing for many of you is the belief that if you do something for your fellows, something will be taken from you. And the belief in scarcity you must attend to before you can know yourselves as truly free and in worth.

If you believe there is only enough food for you, you will not feed your brother. If you understand that the Creator is in manifestation as you and, consequently, you will be supplied by the Source of all that is, you always have enough to share. You have been deprived many things because you were told there would never be enough. And as you agreed to that, you created a system of hoarding and protection in the belief that if there was not enough, you would not be left away from all that you need.

Now we will ask you one thing: What is one thing in your possession that you do not need? What is one thing in the home you live in that you lock away or ignore, that you haven't even thought you could use, and then ask yourself why you attach to it. "It's convenient that it's there." "I don't know what to do with it." "Somebody must have given it to me once." "It used to fit me and now it doesn't." Whatever your reason is, we would want to ask you: Who would benefit from claiming this thing from you? Who would you offer it to? Who may be in welcome to it?

We want you to do this now. Make a list of things you do not need that you hold on to out of a belief in scarcity, that you must have it in your house because something or other could happen to you, and ask yourself if you are willing to leave it at the doorstep of the next place you see that attends to such offerings. You are not giving yourself anything. You are giving it to somebody else so that you may learn once and for all that what moves through you is gifted to all. "Well, I paid the money for it, it's mine," "I don't want to share it," is your right, but when you claim things in this way, you attach to scarcity and you lack inclusiveness.

Why would you not feed your brother? is what we ask you. Why would you not shelter your brother? Why would you not clothe your brother? You must ask yourself these questions. And if you tell yourself, "It is not my responsibility," we would ask you, "What is?" What is your responsibility? What is your responsibility to your neighbor?

If you have worked with our texts, you have been asked to walk down the street and witness everybody before you as an aspect of the Creator in manifestation. Everybody is where they can be given the level of consciousness that they have aligned to. You do not know the lessons they need, or why they came, or what they are required to learn. But you can know that they are here and they have the inheritance you do, and that they are allowed the kingdom.

You do not hand your brother the kingdom. You witness him as being wealthy from it. You see him in his inheritance so he may align to it himself. But that will be his claim. However, you cannot deny that same man a hamburger that you would bless in Christ. The hypocrisy of this has gone on for far too long and those who attend to themselves as religious and decide the merit of another based on a scripture that they do not know or practice is a heresy. If you damn your brother, you have damned yourself. And we underline this: *When you damn your brother, you damn yourself.* When you feed your brother, you are fed. When you love your brother, you are loved.

"Well, I can't love my brother, I don't know him." Yes, you do. When you claim "I know who I am, I know what I am, I know how I serve," you have been given the key to know who he is as well. You are all cut from the same cloth, made of the same frequency, vibrating at different levels. As you align to your worth, you align to your responsibility as the one who may claim himself and his fellows in the kingdom.

Now we ask you this: Who are you to deny yourself this? What level of privilege do you hold that you think this may apply to somebody else and not to you? What have you done, or believed you have done, in this lifetime or any lifetime that could harm you in such a way that you would not be allowed to participate in the celebration that is about to begin? And when we say a celebration is about to begin, we mean that the waking up of mankind to his potential as the divine being he has always been is cause for joy. You are not so shameful, you know.

We will draw the circle again, as we drew before. And the circle, we will say, is the love of the Creator. And you put yourself on the perimeter, right outside of the dividing line. Now invite yourself in. Step over the line. And if you will not, we will do it with you. We will extend the line, redraw the line to include you. There is no being on this planet who is not loved. Understand this, please. And if that is true for the one next to you, that must be true for you as well. But the belief that you cannot be keeps you standing at the gate when the party is going on inside. We open the door, we welcome you in, and we say, "Yes, yes, yes. You have come home. You have come home. You have come home."

The belief that you are not worthy dictates that your fellows must not be worthy as well. And that is where you go into agreement. You can create a hell on earth very quickly this way, you know, and in some ways you have. The denial of your own gifts have caused you to create separation from the gifts that would be given to you. As you claim your inheritance, "I know who I am, I know what I am, I know how I serve," you align to the gifts that would be gifted to you and you move into accordance with them.

We will draw the circle again with you at the center. And on the outline of the circle you will imagine that the abilities you need to demonstrate, to move you forward, are all written out for you. "My ability to learn," "My ability to see," "My ability to know," "My ability to maintain myself in my high vibration." Imagine that these things that you need are just outside the border. Now we draw the circle once again so that they are included in your field. You are the chooser here. This is not just a symbolic act. This is a choice you make to claim yourself in dominion. "In dominion" means in authority, and "in authority" means you are responsible.

Now who are you anyway? What do you think you are? What can you imagine yourself to be? These are all important questions to ask yourselves. And the desires you have to be known by us is simply a reflection of the desire to be known by yourself in your true merit. You are obligated to yourself, first and foremost, to hear your own voice, your own requirements for change and choice. As you listen, you will be taught by yourself and you will move toward these things you need one at a time.

No one is waiting for you, you know, to change. You are the only one here. You are the only one who can decide this. You live your life as you claim it. You are the authority you seek. And as you don't want to be, you find others to fill the role. We are not that role. We are teachers, and any teacher worth merit has one goal in mind: the learning of the student so the student may attend to herself.

As we gift you with the frequency we work with, we do this for one reason: so you may work with yourself and your fellows. "I am Word through my body, I am Word through my vibration, I am Word through my knowing of myself as Word" is the attunement to the frequency we work with. But how you attend to the frequency in your life will always be your claim.

"I am Word through my witnessing of my fellows," "I am Word through my choices," "I am Word through my alignment," "I am Word through my freedom," "I am Word through my love" will support you in claiming these things in your worth. "I am Word through all that I know to be true" will support you in realizing the truth in any and all situations you may encounter. When you claim, "I am Word through all I know to be true," it states very simply that you have moved into resonance with truth and what is not in truth will not be in adherence to your field. It will not resonate with you as truth, so it will fall away. So many choices to make, we say, may be made in a new way once you realize you can. That your choices are made in authority and that you are responsible to your choices.

Why do you choose what you choose, why do you claim what you claim, and why do you keep what you don't need when you can gift it to your fellows? If you would do one thing today—and we will ask you to do this—let go of something you no longer need. Give it to someone who does and only for the sake of your own soul's growth. You are aligning to the new, so you must release the old.

Now, do not decide that this is a punishment, and do not decide that this is a wasteful act. It is a benediction that you give to a fellow when you offer him the food he needs to survive. When the clothes that they wear cannot keep them warm and you have a closet full of clothes, why do you hide them from your fellows? You are the one responsible, you know, for your brother as you attend to your own worth and go into an awareness of his.

We love you each at whatever level of learning you stand in. We accept you each at whatever level of knowledge you may have attained. We understand that for some of you going on this journey is a confusing act because it means defying what you were taught and holding yourself accountable in ways you thought would never have to.

But the days of convenience really are over. And those of you who would claim a spiritual path while leaving your brother on the roadside to starve must wake up to your own accountability. "But they created that," you may say. For whatever reasons you may not know. But if they created that, they have also created the opportunity for you to serve and you must say thank you to them for this gift. You know who you are. Act upon it, please. You cannot bear witness to the perfection in your fellows and not house him, not keep him fed, and not keep him loved.

Now we will stop for today and we will continue soon. We have gifts to give you when we return. Thank you both and good night. Stop now, please.

Day Six

We respond to you as you need to be responded to. Each one of you who reads our text goes into relationship with us as the listener. And as you listen you receive, and as you receive you grow, you enlighten, you respond to yourselves in a higher way. The journey that you are on now is one of manifestation, the manifestation of the self as can be realized in the Christ vibration held in physical form. Now, this is an enormous journey you're on. It's a reclamation of self. It's a triumphant return to who and what you have always been intended to be.

Why have you gone so far from yourselves? Why was it allowed? Why did mankind create for himself the separation from his Source? In fact, you have never been separated. But the density of vibration that you have created and assist in creating and re-creating through thought-forms, through beliefs, through systems of control that have adhered in such a way that moving beyond them has been a process. The process is here now to be received in a new way as we have given you a technique, a way of operating in Source vibration that you may know.

When you claim "I am the Word," you are self-identifying as the aspect of the Creator that can be manifested in form. *Can* be is the operative word here. You are not incarnating in your higher vibration without work on your part. And to believe that we are giving you language that would solve all your problems and move you into a higher dimensional reality without you taking responsibilities for your creations would be misguidance. We would not do that for you. Mankind is responsible for his creations. What you have created is your responsibility and you are being attended to now by us in our authority, who may support you as you grow and change and reclaim your manifestation as the Creator embodied in form.

Now we ask you what it means to be you. We say this again and again. And as you question your worth, who and what you think you are, you may only come to one conclusion: that you are your own creation to the extent that the beliefs that you hold are identifying you in each situation in your life.

If you are the one who believes such and such, that is what you claim and your reality must form to go into agreement with that level of identification. So as you realign to the manifestation of God as you, the true Christ that is you, the aspect of the Creator that may know itself *as* and *through* you, you realign those aspects of the life you have lived so you may move anew, in a new way, to a new height. From the new height, you may see what you have chosen, you may see what you have believed, and you may re-create the self and the world you exist in in accordance with this.

We continue to teach you today about responsibility, but in a different way. We want to bring you grace, and an awareness of what you can hold as you enlighten yourselves through the usherance of our work into your vibration. Now we say this in a way you may understand. "Usherance" is the word, and we are using it intentionally. We usher the frequency forward so you may claim it, and align to it and embody it.

Now, the frequency was always here, you know, but the density of your creations precluded your manifestation. The belief that it could not be so was paramount in creating the wall of separation that you have existed through. The planet is in shift. The frequency of the planet and all things on this planet are being moved upward in consequential vibration. There is a sequence at hand, you see, and that which will no longer hold the truth, that was born in fear, that was born in negativity, that was born in the need to control another, is being released so the true self, the self in honor, in knowing, and in worth may be reborn as you.

You do not negate these aspects of the self, the self that is fearful, that denies herself her worth. You realign them. You re-associate yourself with the higher worth so that negativity no longer requires itself to be primary, to be the one in control, to be the decider of your fate. In some ways, what you are doing is self-identifying *as* your true self in the acknowledgment that those creations you have used to hold your value were born in fear. Once you understand that you have only been frightened of a system of thinking, of a way of perceiving your value, your worth, your worthwhileness in the face of change, you can create anew.

Now the lives that you have lived up until this day were informed by your beliefs and your beliefs hold vibration. So the reliance on the old systems that you have been compelled to continue with are releasing as you go forward. You choose anew, you release what you do not require, and you attune to the new value of your worth as you continue forward.

Now we decide with you today what you can claim. And we want you to imagine, for a moment, that there was one thing you have always valued in yourself. One aspect of you that you have claimed in power, your authority, in whatever area you would choose: The way you sing a song, the way you treat your fellows, the way you think a thought. Whatever it is you give worth to, we want you to imagine that it is expressing itself *as* you. We want you to align yourselves right now to that sense of value, as if that one aspect of you was a chord being played in your resonance. You are radiating and resonating as the one thing you say is worthwhile.

As you do this, you align your frequency to this sense of expression of identity and you will feel how you feel yourself in your value. Do you understand this? You are teaching yourself what it means to be in your value and to know what it feels like to sing your song. Now, once you understand that you choose this, that you can create the method of your expression through aligning your system to it, you may begin to play other chords. You may begin to play a whole symphony in your expression.

Once you understand that the creations you hold are out-pictured by you in consequence to your frequency, and that your frequency is born of thought, and creation responds to thought, you can play a new song and create a new vibration that claims you in its way. You are your music, you know, and your song is your expression.

In the past we have talked about radios. Yes, you are a radio. You produce the song you choose. You are the vehicle for that expression. When you realize, though, that you are more than the vehicle, you are the active expression of it, you move into a new kind of authority. You go into congruence with the manifestation of yourself at this level of knowing and you become a co-creator to the divine plan that is available to you.

Paul is interrupting, "What is this divine plan? I thought we all had choice." You do have choice. And it is a choice, in fact, to align your vibration to the highest chord available to you to play. And as you play that chord, you move into co-resonance with your Creator, that aspect of you that is eternal and knows its expression. In this alignment you are on your soul's path in a higher awareness. If you wish to say divine plan, you may, but you are fulfilling your own destiny.

Now how each of you serves in this manifestation of your

life is predicated on many things. You all have gifts. You all have ways of knowing yourself through what you choose in your worth. The gifts you have been given have been meant to be presented to your fellows in compassion, in worth, in sharing, so that others may benefit from your presence. As you all give your gifts forward as your expression, you align to each other in your worth, and your compassion for your fellows, your realization of their divine inherent worth, is amplified and the world that you live in plays its music in song in perfect ways.

Now each of you has your own song, yes, your own way of being expressed. And we will say this again: *How you serve is how you are expressed as you in perfect ways.* "What are my gifts?" you may ask. "How am I to be responsible for what I don't know?" Where is your love? Where is your passion? Where is your joy? They will always teach you what your worth is, and how you claim your worth will show you how you serve. If you like to paint, go paint; if you like to cook, go cook; if you like to speak, go speak. But you will be in service as yourself as you align to your worth in whatever way is expressed as you in the highest way possible.

We said be a chord, be *in* accord, if you wish. The music that is you when you are in your worth is expressed as you. That is the symphony being played and your whole life will be in accord with it. We asked you before to go into your worth in one way, feel the resonance of that as you, as you claim it, as you feel yourself express as it, and know that this is so.

Now we want to do something new with you. Imagine for a moment that what holds you in your vibration is infinite possibility, that you are surrounded by infinite possibility, that anything that can be expressed can be known by you. Anything that can be thought can be expressed and, consequently, all is available. Now we imagine you in your own potential, in your own vibration, as we see you before us. We see you as an infinite piece of God in vibration, in accord with all your fellows, and the reliance you have had on your history as a way of self-identifying is being released from you as the package of shame, of control, of fear that is has been. Now you say, "What about my good memories?" We are not talking about memory right now. We are talking about identifying *as* your history in such a way that precludes your Divine Self being expressed as you.

We identify you now as you truly are and we go into song with you. We are going to move your vibration to a chord with our own—to a chord, c-h-o-r-d, accord, a-c-c-o-r-d—with our own. We are going to be the music that plays with you. And in our mutual vibration we are going to liberate you from what you thought you were. Your fear self, the small self, the angry self that relies on her fear to show her who she is, is being released *as* you. And as you claim yourself in a new way, that aspect of you realigns to the Christ vibration that you are, you are, you are.

Now the song has begun. As we work on you each in frequency, you must allow this. We cannot do anything without your permission, nor would we want to. You have been gifted with free will, and that includes the ability to keep your stuff even when it makes you suffer. So many of you believe that you will not know yourselves without your pain because you have self-identified as pain. The self-identification as pain perpetuates pain, and pain wants to know itself as you. Fear creates itself. The need of fear is to replicate itself as you. When you claim pain as your identity, that aspect of yourself that aligns to pain only knows himself through his creations as pain. So as we move you upward, we must ask your permission:

> "Am I now willing to be released from a structure of pain that I have used to self-identify myself as? Am I willing now to release myself from the cycle of fear that I have perpetuated because I believed I must? Am I willing now to be received by my Creator in accordance with my true worth, my Christ-born worth, the divine worth that is instilled in me and in all men?

> "As I say yes, I receive. As I say yes, I allow, and as I say yes, I accept my gift from the Source of All That Is: I know who I am, I know what I am, I know how I serve."

Receive, each of you, the love of God through and as your being. You are allowed this, you know, there is no one on this plane who is denied this. There is no one on this plane who is not worthy of the love of God. So let yourself be blessed, let yourself be gifted, and let us receive you as loved.

We know who you are, we are your friends, we are your teachers, and we align to you as you move into your great potential. You are in authority now of your own creations. You have decided this. And as the one who can choose, you choose yourselves, you choose your freedom, you choose your wellbeing, you choose your worth and you sing your song.

We will end this chapter shortly. We have much to teach you still. The end of this chapter will be a benediction to each of you who wishes to receive it. And we are going to sing your song for you now in allowance of your willingness to serve:

As I lift my light to be seen by my fellows,
As I lift my worth to be received by myself,
I align myself to service so that my gifts may be realized,
So that my gifts may be shared, so that my gifts may be
    seen,
And I may accept myself in my divine plan:
A manifestation of the Creator in form, here to sing my
    song for the benefit of all,
I know who I am, I know what I am, I know how I serve.
I am Word, I am Word, I am Word.

We thank you both and good night. Stop now, please.

FOUR

THIS INCARNATION

Day Seven

We have teachings to give you today about what you need, why you need it, and why you don't claim what you want. You all believe you are small, that you are only allowed certain things, and that if you reach too high the whole shelf will fall down on you, if you reach what's on the top shelf. Now we would like you to know this: What is in your authority is what you can imagine. If it is in your imagination, it may be possible. If it is possible, it may be created. If it is created, it may be held in accord with your own vibration.

Now is this possible, that you could be so great that you could reach the top shelf? Well, what's on the top shelf? What is that thing that you see so far beyond you that you may never hold? We will tell you what it is: *It is you in your authority as the one who may choose her own dominion, his own dominion.* You lie to yourselves every day when you say you are not allowed the life that you can have, if you could, you would have it already. Now we will tell you what this means: You believe, on a certain level, that if you place yourself above what you were taught, you will be disappointed, and you cannot handle disappointment, so you create it in the abnegation of your own authority.

Now, how you've been lied to by your lives is by being told that if you want something, you must go out and get it. And you must do, and you must be active, and you must create in action. This is true on the physical plane. On a spiritual plane, on a thought plane, it is not so. What you do is call to you these things that would create the circumstances for your lives to unfold in the ways that you would claim. You like to put the cart before the horse. You like to think that if you are not running after something, you are not doing. In fact, when you are knowing yourself in your true worth—"I know who I am, I know what I am, I know how I serve"—you claim dominion, and what you call to you in your authority is in accordance with the worth that you hold.

The top shelf, we say, the high shelf that you believe to be so out of reach, is something you must lift to in your vibration, not by standing on a ladder made of rickety creations. It will always fail you. What is a rickety creation? A thing that is created in fear. What is a rickety creation? A thing that you require, that you believe you must have to get to the next rung.

When you know you can lift, you do not climb. You invest in climbing, you invest in arduous action in order to get what you want because you cannot imagine that you could be gifted in receipt with what you truly need. Now, why does this get to you? Because you have been taught this way and you agree with it. And you feel that if you are not in agreement with something that you were taught by somebody else, you must be wrong, it must be wrong, it cannot be so.

Now how do you lift, to rise, to the top shelf? Through intention. And, simply said, intention is a creative action that you claim as being so, not "one day will," but being so. "I am Word through this intention" sets the action of the frequency of the Word in consciousness to the circumstance, or situation, or requirement that you need to bring into manifestation. When you are doing this, in accord with your vibration as the one in worth, it will be so.

When you do this from a place of manifestation that says it cannot really be so, you will get what you ask for that way. So what is on the top shelf? You. As you can see your world from a higher vantage point, how you get there is lifting your vibration. What is on the top shelf is what exists in a higher frequency. You think your car lives there. There may be a car there; there may be something finer. Those of you who believe heaven is like a shopping mall will be in great disappointment when you realize, very quickly, that what you invest in in this plane that is not in accord with your worth cannot exist in your vibration once you leave this plane.

As you exist here, you create mountains of stuff that is your legacy that goes to dust the moment you are gone. When you rise in vibration, you claim things in accord with truth because truth lives in high frequency. What is in truth is eternal and you carry that with you throughout your lives.

As you grow as a spiritual being, your legacy is one of love. That is what you become, that is what you claim, that is what you gift to the world. *Who you are is who you say you are.* We will say this many times. "I am the one who is fearful" claims you in fear. "I am the one who knows who he is, who she is, who may live her life in accordance with her new worth as an aspect of the Creator in form" is the legacy you claim in this incarnation. And we will say that will be the title of this chapter, "This Incarnation."

What you have been gifted with, and what you all believe not to be true, is a wonderful opportunity to know who and what you are in all of your encounters. There is no one who encounters you in your life that is not your teacher, that is not there to show you who you are in your own reflection as you engage with them.

Now we will ask you this: Who in your life has taught you the most difficult lessons? Was it your mother, or your father, or the philandering spouse or the ungrateful child? Who taught you the hard lessons? And you must ask them, the lessons themselves, what they were there to teach you. "What did I learn, what did I learn, what did I learn?"

Now Paul is getting in the way. "Well, if she had a philandering husband, she knows she can't trust men." That may be what she claims, but that may not be the truth of the lesson. The truth of the lesson may be much greater. "I know I am worthy of love regardless of the behavior of another." "I know I am worthy of being seen regardless of what I look like to another." "I know that I am worthy of living my life regardless of what I am told by someone who doesn't care anymore." You claim your lessons as a possibility of new industry, new awareness, new life, new choices, new being. But you must say yes to the positive lessons that are brought to you through your interactions. In some ways they are your stepping-stones to new worth.

When you abnegate your worth by believing others are always right—"He must have been right to leave me, I will never amount to much on my own"—you claim your authority in that abnegation of power. And that resonance begins to infiltrate all areas of a life. If you want that, that is up to you; keep plucking things off the low shelf and putting them in your basket if that is what you want, or hear us now: *You are the one who chooses, regardless of what you think or have been taught.* And if you are carrying a handbasket of trash, drop it now. Who is to tell you not to but you? Now, if you want your trash to stick with you, be prepared to stink, because that's what trash tends to do after a while. If you do not want it, you have been given the authority to let go.

Now we will tell you this: Many of you were taught things when you were very small. You believed them implicitly and you created a life to reflect these teachings regardless of whether or not they were serving you well. You were told you were this or that, you were mistreated by this one or that one.

But we are here to tell you now that just because something happened does not mean it has to stay. You have as much authority here, but you don't know it. You have been systematized to agree with the possibility that once you are scarred, you are scarred forever, that once you have been harmed, the memory of the harm will never go away. Well, this is up to you, you know, because, once again you decide what the teaching was.

The teaching may not be what you want to think—it may not be that "my parents were awful," that your life wasn't good—it may be the teaching that you can claim your power back in any circumstance regardless of how challenging it may be.

What you give your authority to becomes your God. And if you want your pain to be your authority, or the memory of your pain, that will be your claim, that is what you put in your basket, that becomes your broadcast, or your resonance and you call it back to you in every moment of your waking life.

We do not teach those who have an investment in maintaining their pain as their identity and there are those of you who have become so attached to your history—"This happened to me when I was five, when I was twenty-five, or fifty-five"—that you stand at the roadside looking at the history, the wreck that was your past, and not walking beyond it. Now if you want to stay there, you may; you have been gifted with free will. But this incarnation is yours to learn though. And the moment you decide that there may be another way to learn, to encounter this history, to move beyond the wreckage, you will, but you must choose it.

We understand pain, you know. We do not blame you, but we do not agree that you have no other choice. And those of you who invest in pain or misery as a way of being may have come to the conclusion, sadly, that this is who you are. In that claim of worth—"I am my misery or my pain"—you conclude your future in this moment. The blessing is that your future may be changed by you in this new worth as you attend to it. Paul is saying, "What new worth?" I know who I am. I am an aspect of the Creator. I am alive to learn. I am alive to choose. I am alive to sing my song in its perfection, or imperfection, or joy, or fury, or however you choose to express yourself. But you are alive. You have a choice. As you have choices, you attend to your choices, you may walk forward and call to you your next lesson.

Now difficult things happen in a lifetime. We are not pretending they do not. We understand that many things happen that cause great pain. There are losses, there are changes, there are challenges that would boggle the mind. But we will also tell you this: Your soul has creations that it requires you to know to move forward and to develop in your choices to express yourself in your higher vibration. You are being given opportunity to grow in every opportunity that is presented to you in the form of a challenge. But you must say yes to the new way of being and no longer attend to that aspect of the self that says,

"Yes, see, it happened again. I will never know love, or peace, or worth."

Every time your worth is challenged by a situation, by a person, it is an opportunity to claim it back. As you align to others' needs as the ones who must tell you who you are, you pretend to be small, you give them permission to decide for you, and you agree with them that you are who they say you are. That is your choice. When you are small it is difficult, but the challenges you greet as a child will, in many ways, inform the choices you may make as a soul in vibration learning her own power, her own wisdom, her own promise in expression.

There is no one on this plane, like it or not, who can tell you who you are with more authority than you. This does not make you special. It means, finally, you have to know yourself because you are the only one who really lives with you, and what do you want to be? How do you frame your expression and how do you live your life in accordance with that you have been taught? You've become so ignorant to your own behaviors—"This is the way it should be because I have always known myself as this," "I have always chosen in accord with what I have been taught so I don't think otherwise"—that you miss the opportunity to decide anew. If you have eggs for breakfast six days a week and on the seventh you have toast, you are choosing that. If you don't want toast, eat something else.

You always claim your worth through your interactions with others, situationally and interpersonally. Where do you deny your worth and why do you do it? Who, we would say, is greater than you? If there is a God, and we will tell you there is, He is manifested in everyone, She is manifested in everyone, if that is your preference. But the manifestation of the Creator instilled in each of you coming into its own recognition is the great teacher. That is the teacher you wish to listen to.

We do not want your authority; we want you in your own. And if we have to pat you on the head, or push you on the bottom to get you moving forward as the one who may claim her choices, we will attend to that as we need to. As you live this life, you are your own teacher regardless of what you think and how you align to possibilities. How you create circumstance in order to teach the lessons you need is the subject of this talk. Your teachers, we say, are what you choose to learn through. Every situation, once again, is an opportunity for new learning, but how do you wish to learn?

If everything is an opportunity to claim your merit, your Divine Self-worth, you have learned the lesson of the day and you may raise your flag and say, "Teacher, I am done for the afternoon." If you wish to stay and say, "My teachers told me life was bad. My circumstances brought me to this place of pain and here I will stay," that is your claim as well. But the moment you decide something new, "I may change, I can change, and my circumstances, which are a reflection of my consciousness, may realign with the new worth I gift to myself as I know myself as I truly am."

How do you know yourself in your days? How are you seen

by your fellows? And how do you perceive yourselves through their eyes? How do they know what they need from you, and where do you presuppose their needs based on your historical changes? "If he looks at me this way, he must want that," "If she says this, it must mean that."

You must understand right now that you are all in agreement with the teachings you require on one level or another. So you bless each other in the opportunity to have certain experiences as your life unfolds. "I will be the mother, I will teach you independence." "I will be the lover, I will teach you your passion." "I will be the child, I will be learning from your worth so I may create my own." You go into these agreements prior to incarnation and you choose them as you go forward, as you recognize each other in spirit, and call each other into being in a practical way in the incarnation you exist in.

Not everything is predetermined. We do not say that. But we do say that you encounter yourself through your fellows in ways that are predetermined, to grant you the opportunity to claim the lessons you came here for. What does it mean to claim a lesson? To agree to it. Now, you may agree to the circumstance or the challenge. "I need to know what it feels like to be the prisoner or the keeper this time around." "I need to know that I am still in my worth regardless of what society has told me." "I need to learn that I can transform myself in ways that amaze me because I know who I am." But these are choices you make to grow. And if you turn down the opportunity for learning that is presented in each of them, you will call the opportunity to you again. There is no shame in this. You may take the test again until you say, "Aha! I know! I understand, and I know that I may move forward in my worth in this new knowledge I have accepted as my own."

Now when there is tragedy or what you perceive to be tragedy, you have a great opportunity to relinquish an aspect of the self that believes she knows, he knows how things are supposed to be. You have records, you know, in your memory banks, of great tragedy that has occurred on this plane throughout time. And you have been emblemized by these memories to go into reactions that you were attuned to at the time of their initial creation. These are the responses that you all agree are inherited by the race. You see the tiger, you know to run. You see the water rising, you build the boat. But as you re-attune to who and what you are and you realize that your vibration is in consort with physical manifestation, you no longer feel victimized by circumstance or by tragedy. You understand that how you interface with any creation is a reflection of your consciousness.

Two people may see the same accident on the highway and have two very different responses: "Oh, I am so glad I was not driving on the road today," or "How can I help that man behind the wheel?" You are always reflecting your consciousness in what you see before you and what you attend to. You have made collective decisions about the realities that you exist in. And we say "realities" intentionally, because three people may share the same room and inhabit three different levels of consciousness and, consequently, their experience of the room and their circumstances may be radically different.

As you attend to your consciousness, as you vibrate in higher knowing and you call to you the things you need to accept your knowing, agree to it, and then move on, your worth is accelerated and your vibration calls to you circumstances that will reflect the new worth you hold. But everybody has an opportunity through each encounter, and how they choose to perceive it to know themselves anew. We are not saying that things do not happen that will cause you pain. We do speak of how you attend to pain in your worth as a lesson you learn.

Many of you get overly attached to your relationships here. You have come to count on them as ways of knowing yourself in your worth. You have come to count on your choices to always lead you where you think you should go. So when something happens that you perceive to be out of your control, your sense of worth is challenged. Somebody goes away, a situation occurs that challenges your safety or your belief in what it means to be safe in your environment. Until you all learn, each one of you, that you are your brother's keeper and that the wars that you create are manifestations of fear, you will not learn this lesson.

Peace is more than possible. It is an intended state of consciousness that you also know in your DNA, or your record, or whatever you would like to call your history-memory of the race. Peace is more than possible. It can be. But it must be within you to be reflected elsewhere. And we will say this once

again: There is nothing within you that is not projected outward in your expression, and what you fear within yourself,
you fear within your fellows, you fear within your world, and
when you are frightened of your fellows, you move away, and
your need for peace becomes an opportunity for separation
and isolation.

As you create anew, a new possibility of expressing yourself,
you create the same possibility in everybody around you. This
is resonance. As you recognize your worth, as you surmount a
challenge in this incarnation, you give permission to everyone
to do the same. You create a new possibility in your energy field
that others may witness, may know, may see as possible and
they may align to it and call it into being for themselves.

The work you are attending to through the interaction with
us, the guides that dictate the answers you seek, or pose the
questions you wish not to hear, are for everyone. The answers
you seek are implicit in the questions you ask. As everyone
moves up to the higher level of being, which we will say can be,
can be, can be, can be—there is no top shelf, there is just where
you stand in recognition of the ones beside you in a shared creation of love.

Now, this sounds fanciful to Paul, and he doesn't like the
word "love," "shared creation of love." It sounds a little silly to
him, but he has emblemized love to be something that it is not.
When you are in awareness of your own worth in a productive
way, you may call this self-love. When you are in awareness of
the worth of your fellows, you may share your love with them

freely and without fear. When there are many in love, that is a
shared creation. You must acknowledge the worth, the inherent worth, of all men, regardless of what you think of them, to
truly attend to this teaching. And if you have already decided
that there is someone who cannot be forgiven, you have tried
and decided that this is not for you. But we will offer you this:
When you remember the one before you, regardless of what he
has done, how he has hurt you, what she has destroyed, and you
remember this being as on her own road to learning, his own
road to discovery, you become a bit more compassionate.

What have you done in your lives that you believe you cannot be forgiven for? That is an act of arrogance, you know, and
you may accept that in a certain way by looking at the one next
to you and deciding that it is safe for her to be forgiven for what
she believes she has done or may have, in fact, done. All forgiveness is, we will say, is a releasing of fear. When you release
the fear of another, they may be in forgiveness as well, and you
may move to a new vibration in the light of love.

Now we will offer you this: This teaching for the day, "Incarnation," is about responsibility to how you attend to your
lessons as the one in choice. If everything is an opportunity for
growth, what are two challenges you face today in your life,
environment, family, relationships, anywhere? What are two
challenges you face and how might you claim your worth
within them? How might you decide anew in a place to bring
you to a higher level of knowing? How might you attend to
each lesson in a productive way that will not keep you in fear,

or in languishing or blame? How might you grow? What is the opportunity being presented to you in this circumstance, and how might you go forward in attendance to it?

We offer you this: If you attend to these two things today, we will support you as we can by illumining this thing as you allow us to show you the new possibility that you may call to yourself in your relationship to the situation, or the person, or the thing. If you invite us to work with you to illumine the new possibility, you must be prepared for the possibility you will not like it, because it will mean you have to change something you initially invested in that made you party to the creation in the first place. Do you understand this?

You are party to all of your creations. You are part of the creation because you are in resonance with it. And as the one in resonance with it, you are participatory in an exchange of vibration. So re-creating something, in a new way, in many ways, means you need to turn the dial, to change the station, or the accord that you have with the circumstance that you would like to transform. We hope you understand this. You cannot change something the same way that you create it. You need a new thought or a new possibility to lift you to the next level of thought and vibration that may transform something that you have known and agreed to historically.

Now each one of you has decisions to make about the life that you live. The choices you will make as you attend to this text will be different than you think. The choices that you make when you are in agreement to your worth may challenge you at times to prove this to yourself: to honor the choice that you make as the one who knows who she is, what she is, how she serves, is the lesson you will have. As you grow up, you see the higher shelf before you, and eventually you are lifted to the place where that thing you have sought is standing right before you, right at your eyes, at the level of your eyes, to be seen and welcomed.

We offer you this in love, and we tell you why. We know your worth already. You do not have to prove it to us. You have to do nothing but attend to those aspects of the self that disregard their worth and create in their fear of being who they think they should be.

You have been told who you were all your lives. Most of you have agreed with what you were taught. Now we will tell you this. We are only telling you what we know. How you attend to your own information must be through your own experience of this text, the teachings and what they take you to next. As you honor this, you become your own authority and it is only in your own authority that you may claim your worth.

We will stop in a moment for this day. We would like to say one last thing about cherishing. What you cherish is something that you are aligned to, in one way or another. What you cherish, you hold. Can you imagine, for a moment, if you were the thing to be cherished, exactly as you are, in this moment in time, exactly as you stand before yourself? May you still be treasured, may you be cherished, may you be known in love.

If you will allow us now, we will surround you in love and we will open your frequency to a whisper:

You are loved, regardless of what you have been taught, how you have been treated, how you have treated yourself. You are deeply loved as are all men, as are all women, as are all. Simply allow, right now, the self to receive and to be still and know.

I know who you are, I know what you are, I know how you serve. And I am one with the power that I am with in frequency, in love, and in my own worth.

Thank you and good night. Stop now, please.

Day Eight

We respond to the needs of the time first, and Paul, you have an issue that needs to be rectified before channeling can continue. Your anger at others is coming forward to be addressed and you dislike the feeling and you decide you cannot have anger and you suppress what you feel. You deny yourself and the anger turns inward and that is a cycle of predisposition to depression.

Now we will offer you this: If you wish to do the work here in this vicinity while you are together,[3] you may, but not before you attend to the reason you are angry. You don't know the reason you are angry and you don't believe it when we tell you

---

3 Paul and Victoria were together in the same room for this session.

your anger is at yourself for not being the one in charge of what you think you are in charge of, of not being able to control others as you wish them to be controlled. Now, you are not alone in this. Everybody has this issue. But others are quicker to forgive. Others are quicker to forgive themselves and to forgive their fellows.

Now, why is it you are not forgiving? Why does one not forgive? Because one is frightened of what will happen if one forgives. "I will be harmed again." "I will be slandered." "I will be judged." "I will be persecuted." "I will be used." You have a long list, as everybody does, of reasons you must not forgive. But the ideal of forgiveness as we have expressed in previous teachings is to release the one that you hold hostage and bind yourself to. As you are willing to forgive, you may indeed be forgiven and the chapter that we would teach, on forgiveness perhaps, would come forward easily. We can only work with you as you allow yourself to be worked through. We cannot control you, nor do we intend to. This book will be completed, we promise you this. But not before you forgive yourself and your fellows for what you believe they have done.

Now, when you decide that you cannot be forgiven, that you are not allowed forgiveness, you entrench yourself in a belief system that you are stuck in and cannot be changed. Not to forgive is to keep something static that seeks movement. To release something to its freedom is required. To stay in your power as the one who knows what she needs is a requirement.

Now you will ask yourself this: Why do you deny forgiveness? Why is the claim on you and your fellows one to first judge and then decide if it is safe to offer forgiveness to? When you offer yourself in forgiveness, you give others opportunities to forgive you as well. When you judge yourself and give yourself permission to close a door on forgiveness, you decide in advance that there will be no forgiveness and, consequently, no movement.

Now, the damage you each do to yourselves through this action or, if you would like to say, inaction, is surmountable and there is an easy way to forgive, if you will allow it, and this is to give peace, to offer peace, to claim peace in the rage, to decide in peace where there has been frustration impressed upon a situation. To deny the self, this entrenches the self. To deny this for your fellows entrenches your fellows in the same response. If you wish to move the response, you may, but you must first attend to the self.

"I know who I am, I know what I am, I know how I serve" will align you to peace, if you allow it. And we must underline this, *if you allow it.* If you bring peace to a situation from deciding that you can allow it, you will claim peace. And as you claim peace, you express peace and you call peace to you, and that is what happens very easily as you decide you can be forgiven for judging yourself so harshly. You may decide this for your fellows as well.

Now of course we are teaching through you, Paul, because we are trying to get you to learn. As you exhibit your frustrations on those you encounter, you damn them in your own way. Do you understand this? When you are frustrated with somebody else for not adhering to what you think they should do, you are condemning them in your own way. And what gives you the right to decide for your fellows how they should be, what they must know, how they must live their lives?

Now of course you may act in an awareness of others' behavior. You may discern what is healthy and what is not for you to be in an encounter with. You may decide for yourself to maintain a friendship or to move on from it. But to condemn another, which is to decide for them and put a lid on the jar that they are in as you express yourself in authority as the one to do so, keeps them in that space in your objectification of them. They may be free as a bird in their own lives, but you hold them in this way, in your own decision about them, and you hold yourself in place as their judge.

You all must understand that all that you encounter is, indeed, a reflection of your worth and when you encounter something or someone that does not merit you, that does not give you your own power, you must first ask yourself why you do not allow your own power to be perceived. Where do you have an investment still in hiding your light or seeking to claim your worth through the approval and decisions of others? If anybody can take away your worth from you, it was never yours to begin with. Do you understand this, yes? This is a very important teaching. Nobody can take your worth from you and nobody can grant it to you but you.

The games you play with your fellows of who is higher and

who is lower, who has this and who has that, are all temporary means of interacting based in a status quo that you have ascribed power to. It has no other power other than what you have ascribed to it. It is an illusion. It is an illusion that one may be better than another or perceived as such.

In the final reckoning, you know, not only are you all equal but you are seen in your truth. And your truth, we will say, is naked and unencumbered by the things that you have amassed in this world that you use to give you power or the illusion of it. The weapons that you yield and the shields that you use to protect yourselves from your fellows are all gone and you stand with your arms extended in an awareness of who and what you have been.

Now why do you need to forgive yourselves? You must forgive yourself, you know, for not knowing any better than you did at the time that you make something so. If you can do this much, you can release yourself from a magnitude of contention that you have created against the self. If you decide, right now, that every choice that you have ever made was born in awareness that you held at the moment that choice was made, you can be understanding of the way that you operated and when. If you knew now what you knew then, you may well have done differently, but you cannot know, you cannot claim what you do not know. Do you understand this, yes?

So you offer yourself forgiveness by allowing for the mind to accept that its own choice was made in an understanding of a possibility that was born at a certain level of consciousness that you have moved beyond now. But to punish the self again and again, for a thing thought, a deed done, an action taken, is to harm the self again and again and the re-enactment of this creates damage not only to you but for those that you encounter.

Now when you offer yourself forgiveness, you must appeal to the possibility that everybody else, regardless of what you think of them, was in the same boat, choosing as they knew how based in the information they held born in their history, in the structures that they have attended to. As you respond to your own needs as one who may be forgiven, you also extend this to those around you. You cannot keep one thing hidden. You cannot keep one crime unforgiven. You might as well keep the whole thing. Do you understand this? If you have one dollar in the bank, you still have an account. When you empty the account, you no longer have it, you are free. So why do you invest, still, in those actions that would claim you back, that would call you back to your history again and again and again?

There is an aspect of you, Paul, that takes pleasure in suffering. You grew up sad enough to underscore the possibility that you believe that this was who you are. And that attendance has been something that we have worked with you on effortfully for many years, and the lifting that you have done in your own vibration in support of others is a testament to this. But the memory that you hold of having been harmed and the frames that you have created that protect you from future harm are what you are attending to now.

You must understand, each of you, that when you keep a frame and you keep it handy, a way of seeing the world will be made to fit the frame. The world that you hold before you is always conforming to the frame that you hold before you. So when you release that frame, you allow the new possibility to come forward. When you revert to your history, in fact what you are doing is re-creating an old frame and aligning your history to your future creations. Of course it must fit the frame. You have created the frame. You are intending that frame to be filled by what you have known.

Now, how do you move beyond a lifetime of shame, of fear, of living in ways that were not for your highest good? Can a human being, in fact, be repatterned, be reborn in their own higher knowing to a peaceful way of existing? Is this possible, or is this illusion? We will tell you this: It is not only possible; it is the work we do with you, that we do with each of you as you align to us. The intention that you hold that it may be possible is what allows this to be. But the history that you have known, that you grab and you hold on to for the safety of the known is often more of a comfort than what you cannot fully hold because it has not made itself fully present, is what you are encountering when you wish to say no.

Now we say yes, it can be, it is so, for the simple reason that mankind's true essence is to be expressed in love, in freedom, in choice, and in gratitude for all that has been gifted to him. If you can be in gratitude, if you can move your awareness to a place of wonder, to new possibilities, you will, you will, you will claim them and call them to you. But you must trust the possibility that this is happening even when you cannot see it. Even when it is not seen, it is so. The sun is alight somewhere when all you perceive is darkness. You can understand this. The sun is shining somewhere and you must see the sun as in its return in the darkest moments of your life.

As you are taught by your creations, your creations being those things that you have chosen to learn through, you encounter yourself in each interaction. And as you learn who you are, as you are re-created through these encounters, you claim an ideal, an identity of who and what you say you are. But nothing that you choose is infinite because your soul knows better than you do. What you choose in fear may be re-created in love. What you have known in pain may one day be known in love. What you have been imprisoned by may, indeed, be the way you find your freedom.

You must understand, you all must understand, that the crimes you do against yourselves are infinitely worse than the crimes you do against your fellows. And the crimes you do against your fellows could only be made so by one who had done it to himself in one way or another. Everything is expressed outwardly, finally, that is born in a creation inside. We do not demand you change. We offer you the hands to hold. We walk you to the light in whatever way we can, however you allow us to, however you say, *we will come.* And we assure you of this: There is no one who calls our name, "I know who I am, I know what I am, I know how I serve," that is not attended to in love.

Paul is saying, "What does this mean, our name—I know who I am?" I am who I say I am, and I know what I am. And as I know, I encounter you in your worth. There is no Christ but you. There is no Christ but me. There is only Christ in the manifestation of God and seeded in each of you. It has come to be, it has come to be, it has come to be.

Now what do you want? Why do you want your pain? Why do you believe that it is necessary to live a life in suffering? You must ask yourself these questions. You must decide, each of you, that you are allowed, that you are safe in your choice to change. But in that choice you must claim power: "I know I am in a new possibility. I know I am in a new choice. And I will trust even though I do not see the light that will come to me when I know what I am."

We will tell you this, Paul. You are a teacher of the Word. And there are many teachers of the Word coming into their own awareness through these times of change. A teacher of the Word is a teacher of embodiment. The Christ has come in man to be expressed as man as man aligns to the vibration of it. But when you decide in advance that you cannot be forgiven, or he or she cannot, you close that door until you are willing to open it again. When you judge your fellows, you judge yourself. And we have said this many times: What you judge, you fear. So why do you fear yourselves and why won't you allow us to teach you a new way: a new way to be, to freedom, to sing, to align, to create, and to know who and what you are?

Now we will tell you this, Paul: We are not impatient with

your process. We are very patient with you, as we are patient with all of our students. We understand that your histories inform your daily lives, and the surrendering to the new feels, at times, impossible when the shadows of the old creep upon you and tap you on the shoulder and say, "Don't forget us." You will not forget them. You will not need to know them anymore because the light that you hold as you claim your vibration in truth and create a consciousness in this intention, "I am Word," you will align to the new, and the old will not be permitted to that level of creation.

Now the walk that you are on, and the walk that you are each on, has been prescribed by your soul in your own awareness of your worth. The teaching you are being given now of worth and knowing is to support you in accelerating this process in significant ways. The trajectory you are choosing is one to benefit not only you but all that you encounter. And the choice to sing, to be your frequency in full incarnation, is what we are attending to now.

We will ask you this: Do you, Paul, do you, the reader, or the listener, or the student of this text wish to take the next step with us? If you say "Yes," and you mean this from your heart, we will lift you, and we will lift you to a way of encountering the self that will be both frightening and wondrous. And by this we mean to say that your true reflection will be seen by you as you have accepted it, as you have been treated and as you have decided. And as you see what you have created, the mask that you have claimed will be withdrawn for you, but you cannot see beyond it until you first see that you still wear a mask. So the exposure may be frightening for you, but what you will understand very soon is that what lies beneath that mask is more wonderful than you could have ever imagined.

You all are protecting yourselves from your own beauty, from your own light, and from your own infinite design. As you release the safety that you have known, as you say "Yes" to this possibility, the bells will ring and the resonance of the bells will be the song you hear and that you attend to. We say the decision is yours. What do you want? If you want this, say "Yes," and say it now, and we will return shortly with the news of the day.

We thank you for your attentions tonight. We thank you for your willingness to sit. We thank you for your willingness to listen and to hear. As we say good night, we say we have heard you say "Yes," and we will attend to you each in this night as you align to us and give us permission to shake you up, to lose the pain, to bring the world anew, to a new way of being as you, as you, as you.

We thank you each. Stop now, please.

II

FIVE

THE PRECIPICE

Day Nine

We would like you to know things about why you do what you do unconsciously, why you make choices that you don't understand, and why you don't consider the options that may be made available to you if you learn to trust yourself in a true way. Many of you act on principle, "This is the right thing to do," "This is the wrong thing to do," but you do not consider that principles are inherited behavior. You do not ask yourself why you adhere to them because you were told not to ask. Now, we are not telling you not to do things in a certain way that you have become accustomed to. But we are also telling you that you must know that when you act in principle without understanding why you are doing what you are doing, you are merely adhering to your history.

Now we will explain this: When you have been told not to tell a lie, you don't tell a lie. You don't not tell a lie because if you understand that you are creating. . . .

. . .

(Interruption)

We will ask you now to stop fighting this,[4] and allow the transmission to come as it wishes. We are the authors of this text, we have things to say, and we know what we want to say without interference. This is not a mandate; it's a decision we make that the transmissions we bring through you will be clear and responsible. By "responsible," we mean in order, and as needed for the reader to learn the lessons we bring them. We know what we do when we teach and we do not need anybody in the background saying, "Will this happen today?" You have enough experience with us to trust the transmission as it wants to come through.

Now today we are teaching you about principles and those things that you adhere to because you were taught as such. "I will not tell a lie," when that is in your principle, is all well and good, but if you do not know why you adhere to this principle, you are acting pro forma, in obligation to your history.

Now, each of you knows things that are true. "I am in a male body. I live in a house on Main Street. I have a child named Bill and a wife named Mary" and you feel fine about those truths. You don't question those truths because they are presented before you. But why is it wise to always tell the truth? Why is it

---

4 This is directed to Paul, who has been thrown by the interruption to the channeling.

true to be in your worth regardless of what is said about you? Why do you adhere to these things without question?

Now we will tell you one thing: You are the one choosing every day of your lives. And what you need to know to bring yourself forward you call to you, you claim and you say "Yes" and you allow it to be there. When you tell a lie, you are always frightened. We have said this many times. When somebody tells you it is not right to tell a lie, they are probably telling you to behave, and that is a very different thing. To behave is to be in agreement with what people tell you you should be, and there is no merit there if it is not born in your integrity and in your worth.

Those of you who decide that such and such is right, and so and so is wrong because you have an *idea* about them are lying to yourselves. You are not the expert in others' worth, only to tell them they are there because they are meant to be there. Their need, your need, everyone's need is to be expressed in their worth. And as you judge your fellows, you continue to judge yourself.

Now today we would like to teach you some things about your obligations, your adherence to forms, and those things that you think are so that may be so or may not be so. The alignment that you each have to date brings you to where you stand. There can be nothing in your reality, for better or for worse, that you cannot agree with. So, consequently, how do you choose what you call to you as your inheritance—your inheritance being your worth as expressed by you in all ways?

The decisions that you make that are born in form, that are born in agreement with history, continue to perpetuate what you have known. The willingness that you must each take now to go forward is to realize that when you walk toward the unknown, you must align to it as a place of infinite choice.

How do I live in infinite choice? Where do I go when the map I have called to me for the rest of my life no longer serves me anymore? How do I stand in my knowing when my authority is questioned? When the rules that I believe were told to me for a good reason may only be there to get me to behave?

Now you ask yourself these questions and you lie to yourself when you pretend you don't know the answer. You know who you are. You are an aspect of the Creator manifested in form and the decision to be this in actions, in your words, in your deeds, will claim you in your worth as the one who may know what she needs. What is infinite worth but a true statement of each man and woman as they are designed and protected by the light that they are?

Paul is having issues today and they are large issues. He is disassembling the channeling as it comes through him and it makes it very difficult to transmit clearly. He is angry today, he has been angry for days, and anger does not serve our work. So we will continue as we may and we will decide as we continue if we will include this chapter in our text. It gives us a reason to talk to him directly and it also gives us purpose to move him through this so he may be of better effect.

The designs you have held and known as your own have

been agreements you have made with your history. The contracts you have signed, the decisions you made to be this way or that way, were agreements you made born in your history. Now why do you want to do this all the time? Why do you claim this for yourself? Why do you bring this upon you again and again? Because you think you must and because you do not know that there are other ways to be.

Now, if you want to lie to yourself and tell yourself that you are not in choice, you may go back to bed, you may go back to sleep, and you may stay there. There is no reason to read further. But if you can align to the possibility, each and every one of you, that you stand at the precipice of great change, of infinite possibility, the moment you are willing to relinquish who and what you thought you were supposed to be to become who and what you are, you will see that the cliff that you stand on the edge of is the launching pad for the rest of your life.

You each choose this, you know. You crawl to the cliff and you expect an arduous climb. Things are only as arduous as you make them. And if you don't want to climb, allow yourself to be lifted. You each have choices, you know, about who and what you are and how you live your lives.

Now we will answer a question that Paul has been having about the last dictation we gave you. It is the end of the previous chapter; it is not included in this one. This is a new chapter on your responsibility to all of your entitlements. "All of your entitlements" being all of those things you claim as your own, and that includes those things you would rather not have. If you have them, they are yours. You have claimed them. If you are willing to let them go, we will give you the opportunity to do so today, but it must be done in choice. We do not take things from you that you do not wish to hold. We can only help you to let go so you may release of your own accord.

Now you ask yourself, "What things do I hold that I no longer cherish, that I no longer align to?" and it should not be very hard to create a list of things that no longer serve you. It may not be an easy list to make, but you must understand that by making the list, you are giving yourself permission to see yourself and to see yourself clearly. "I see myself as the one who created this and that," "I see myself as cherishing this pain," "As owning this decision that I made that I no longer want," "That I am claiming my worth as the one who made the error so that I may rectify the mistake." If you don't claim the error, how can you make a new choice? How can you decide anew when you are pretending you are not who you are?

Now understand this please: You are not an error. We don't say that you are an error. But you have made mistakes in your judgment because you have been frightened of yourselves and you have given permission to the world to tell you who and what you are. "I am the woman who lies." "I am the man who cheats at cards," "Who is an infidel," "Who is boastful." Whatever it is you claim as yourself that you wish to relinquish you may, but you must release the need for these things. There is nothing that you have created in your life, including your pain, that you have not chosen for one reason or another.

Now, we do not say that things don't happen to you that
cause pain. We are talking about holding on to pain, cherishing pain, going into agreement with pain as who you are, and
that is not a requirement for being alive unless you make it so.

"I no longer wish to be alone," you may say. But you have
created a life of loneliness and, in fact, cannot imagine another
way of being seen. "I have created a life by myself. I cherish my
time alone. When somebody comes to visit, I cannot wait for
them to leave" may be closer to the truth for you. But you pretend you want a partner, or a lover, or somebody who comes
and stays because you think you should have this.

Now, you may have this if you like, but you will not claim it
as long as you are claiming what you've had is what you want.
And understand, everybody, please, what you have is what you
want because you accept it as so. You may change your mind,
you know. You are allowed to change your mind and to decide
anew any day of the week.

Now we get worried sometimes, when we reach you, that
you misunderstand our teaching, that we are telling you that
you think you caused your pain, and then you use that as an
excuse to harm yourself once again. That is not our teaching.
But our teaching is very clear. You have choice. What you
claim, you hold and are in accord with. What you hold is your
frequency and aligns you to a reality that out-pictures the very
thing you say you don't want. So how can it be not your choice?

As you realign your vibration, as you go through this process we teach you today, you realize how lonely you have been

for yourselves, for your true selves, to come into embodiment to be expressed in their fullness. How lonely you have been for your own love, for your own self-worth to be made known to you. Can this be so? Of course. Can it be so now? Yes. Is it so now, yes! Yes, it is so now, in a higher level of vibration where you already know who and what you are. There is an aspect of you here and now that claims her worth, that sings her song, that rejoices in the fact that she is alive, even if that's not your experience of yourself today.

Now how do we bring this down into your being? By this choice:

> "On this day I choose to align my self-worth and my true self as a Created Being into the manifestation of my body to be expressed in my reality in a way that I may expect to see. I claim my power back from all those creations that have decided for me, that I have gone into agreement with and I have chosen of my own accord to keep me in limitation. I give myself the freedom to be in liberation, to be in this powerful place of knowing who I am. I claim this in my own choice as I say these words: I know who I am, I know what I am, I know how I serve. I am Word through this intention. Word I am Word."

Now, the delineation of responsibilities is what we must take up with you now. You are not responsible for everything, you know. You may ask for help. You may offer yourself as a vehicle of the Christ, as the Divine Self that you truly are. To be in offering means to give yourself over in a supplicatory way to the great power that is you, the manifestation of God that would be expressed through you. You are not bowing down to a statue. You are not paying penance for something you have done in the past. You are simply supporting yourself in this offering by the realization that you are carried forward by the divine as you offer yourself in service to it. You can only be anointed by love, you know. You can only be anointed in your worth, and you may only choose in accordance with your own purpose when you offer yourself to serve.

How do you offer yourself to serve? By realizing once and for all that the being that you are is an aspect of the Creator manifested here and now who seeks to realize herself, himself, in all ways, in all ways, in all ways. The divine aspect of you, come forward as you, claims her opportunities to be in service to those before her, offers herself to the situations that she may lift in vibration, and sings her song to others so that they may learn the words to their own song. You do not deny yourself by doing this. You align yourself by offering yourself. And you align yourself to that aspect of you that knows who she is already.

We must say this for a final time: We are not making you something that you are not. We are claiming you as you are, as you have always been in one way. The eternal you who has come to be known for you, through you, by you, and as you has never forgotten her name. "I know who I am, I know what I am,

I know how I serve" is the song you now sing, and you offer yourself to the possibilities, the infinite possibilities, as we have said, that will be presented to you as you know your worth.

As you align to yourself in this way, you become a trajectory, a vibration that reaches outward, that benefits all that you encounter. Through your actions, through your choices, and through your own liberation you may shake the cages of everybody else so that they may know that they don't need to be in a cage anymore, and they will find their own key to open their own door through your presence. You don't have to tell anybody what to do. When you are operating in the light and in high vibration, you are offering yourself to serve. The work is done through you in the way that is needed in every situation that you may encounter.

Now you deny yourself your light. You pretend you are not worthy. The things that you believe you have done may never be forgiven. The choices may never be rectified. But how can you say these words to yourself when they have brought you to this place of choice? And choice, we say, is always a free thing. When you have a choice, you are free. How can you deny yourself this choice you are making now?

We spoke to you, the last time we spoke, about a mask that inhibited your true expression, and the beliefs that you hold that keep you in adherence to the past, the principles that you've accepted as laws that must now be questioned, the identity that you have claimed to appease others, to make yourself accepted by them must be seen for what they are: a mask that you hold that precludes your beauty from expressing itself in fullness.

Now, when you are driving down the highway and you see a sign that says there's a speed limit of fifty miles an hour, you decide to go into agreement with that sign, for your own safety, perhaps, because you would like to think that everybody else is doing the same thing. And that is a mutual agreement you have made to keep yourself safe on a highway. When you see something that you don't like and you make a decision about it born in your history—"He looked at me that way, he must want something I don't want to give him"—you are aligning to a fear, you are aligning to a belief, and you are creating a choice that you are expressing as your vibration.

You tell the truth because you want to tell the truth. You tell the truth because telling the truth lifts your vibration. You do not tell the truth to harm your fellows. You must be watchful of hiding your motives. Some of you are very good at deceiving yourselves. But when you adhere to form and you don't question a form, you are adhering to your history.

Now the free woman that you are today, the free man that you are right now, has things he must do, and doing these things, we say, in accordance with your worth will give you a foundation that you may stand upon. Every time you take an action on your own behalf, every time you deny fear its purview and stand in your power, every time you align a conscious choice to a new possibility of freedom, you give yourself praise. And to give oneself praise means you lift your frequency in accord with the divine. You are not praising the personality self, you are lifting your vibration. When you give praise to the Christ, you are aligning your frequency to the Christ, so it may lift you as well. That aspect of you that is the Christ, "I know who I am, what I am, how I serve," will always respond.

The delineations we have spoken of are always in choice. Who do you listen to? Who do you honor? What do you believe and why do you choose what you choose? You are the only one who can ask these questions of the self. You are the only one that can know the answers once you ask them. But if you are not poised at the precipice, you will never fly. If you know what you have known and you call yourself back to what you have known because it is safe, you will get what you have gotten and no more.

You stand right now at an end of all you have known. You stand at this ending with one choice in mind: I am now claiming my worth as a divine being born into his knowing, in response to the Creator within him. I choose my life, I claim my worth, and I accept the offering that is gifted to me as I say these words:

"I stand on a precipice of great change. I stand on the edge of truth. I stand on the edge of freedom. I stand on the edge of all that I have known and believed to be true. I stand on the edge of my limitations. I stand on the edge of my fear. And as I say yes, as I say yes, as I say yes, I step forward into the unknown."

We will ask you to do this with us now. Each and every one of you who holds this text in your hands, who hears these words aloud or in your mind:

> "I say yes to the journey before me and I step forward into the unknown."

We are greeting you each as you make this choice. You will be surrounded by us now and received by us in love. We are making you new, we are making you new, we are making you new.

Now we have gifted you with this today in this chapter we entitle "The Precipice." And we say this to you: When we return, there will be changes. We thank you for your patience with the channel and we thank ourselves for staying here to teach in spite of some resistance. We are grateful for the opportunity to teach and we sing your song with you. Good night.

Stop now, please.

SIX

WISDOM

Day Ten

We are pleased to be resuming the sessions. And we offer you this: The lives that you lead will now be informed by choice of a new way of thinking, a new way of deciding, a new way of aligning your choices to wisdom. And wisdom, we say, is the inheritance you are being gifted with today. When we speak of wisdom, we don't speak of your intelligence. We speak of an inner knowing that is inherited by you through the vehicle you stand in, the energy bodies and the physical body that transmits the frequency through you so you may be in your own knowing in a new way.

Now, a new way, we say, is necessary, for you're reliant on the old self to tell you everything still, and that is where the problems occur. When you hear the old self call your name, "You should have done it this way," "It could have been done that way," you run backward and you sort through all your old information to see what you could have done differently and you end up doing the same damn thing you've always done.

Now understand this, please: When you are awakened in a new way, the vision is changed. When the vision is changed, the possibilities are new. When the possibilities are new, there are new choices to call to you. But to be in your wisdom means you identify what you need in a thoughtful, kind way and you inherit your wisdom; you claim the magnificence as the one who may know.

Now, when we speak of knowing, as we have explained previously, we do not speak of thinking. Thinking is a process. It's a sorting. It's a way of managing information. And you may come to a decision through thinking anytime you need to. Wisdom is inheritance of a divine sense of authority. When one is in his wisdom, he is a benefactor to others because he may share information from a higher level.

Now wisdom and information are not always the same thing. Information may be, "What's the telephone number to the store I need to go to?" Wisdom is "Who am I? How do I stand here and be in my knowing and my worth?" And the answer that you receive, that you claim as your own, is in your authority as the one who may claim his inheritance as wisdom.

Now we are speaking in a new way, "as wisdom." And if you can understand what we mean, when you claim yourself as wisdom, you are simply moving into congruence with the frequency of wisdom that is all around you everywhere. You are so used to thinking that it's all about you that you forget that you can access information and conscious thought and the requirements for your needs by intention. When you go into intention with something, you go into alignment with it. And in alignment with it, you are in agreement, you are accessing, you are the receiver and the broadcast of the thing you have claimed.

Now why wisdom? Why do we use that word today? Because when one is wise, one is in their knowing. When one is wise, one may support another. When one is wise, one may trust their information as they accept it. If you wish to be wise, decide you are and move into alignment with all the wisdom that there is.

Now, moving into alignment is not a hard process. It's simply a choice and a requirement that you create to shift your frequency to another level of information and access. When you say you are your name, you align to your name. "I am wisdom" moves your frequency into accord with the frequency of wisdom that will be of benefit to others.

Now, speaking the words will not do it. And you must understand the difference between setting an intention in language only and setting an intention in your spirit. When you shift your vibration in a new way, there is an experience, an overlay that occurs because you are moving your vibration from one space to another and, in the new space, acclimating to the vibration that exists there. So this is experiential, yes. But just to say the words and not to acclimate, not to bring your vibration to the new place, will not support you well.

Now we will ask you this: What is one thing you need to know? Now, don't ask where you left your keys. You probably left them in your bag anyway, or on the place you always leave them. Ask what you need to know in your worth. "Am I the man I believe I am to be in this lifetime? Am I living the life that is in all my possibilities? Am I allowing myself freedom in true ways? Am I trusting myself enough to give myself the promise of a new way of being in my own way, expressed as me, *I know who I am?*"

Now we ask you this: If you ask the question of yourself and you state it as an intention, "I am now asking myself in a higher way to move into alignment with the question I have asked," and you set it as an intention, "I am setting this intention to move my frequency into accord with the response I require to know my own wisdom, my information in the highest way available to me," you will claim it. As you make the intention, you must understand that you are making a decision to align to something. That is very different than grabbing something or shielding yourself from something. It is simply *aligning* to something new. And in this alignment you call your frequency as yourself in this new way.

Now you authorize this. You call it to yourself and, as you go into union with it, you allow the process to commence. Does this mean you will know automatically? If there are obstructions and things you need to sort through to be able to access your wisdom, you have engaged in a process. If you have benefited from our work thus far and are available to this in the way we describe, the instantaneous information may well be available to you.

> "I am aligning to the question and the response that I require. I am Word though this intention. Word I am Word."

Now, as you do this, you must be very careful not to tap yourself on the back and say, "I know the real answer. It is what I want to hear," because you will deceive yourself very quickly.

The alignment that you are calling will operate *as you*. Now you must understand this: "as you" is the key word. "I am in my wisdom," "I am aligned to wisdom," "I am wisdom," if you wish, brings you into alignment with the information you need in your knowing. You are simply the conduit. You are asking and receiving through alignment to the question *as* wisdom and moving to the answer as you align to the answer. It's a shift of vibration, period.

Now, when Paul works with others, he steps into their field, he doesn't go hunting. When he steps into the field of someone, they tell him what their requirements are. The act of receptivity becomes very important so that you may learn. What is it to be receptive, you may ask yourself? To be in allowance. We have spoken of welcome already in this chapter, in this book that we are producing through you, Paul. But we will ask you this, you and the reader. Do you understand what we mean? The allowance of information simply means that you are the receptor and the vehicle of the expression. You are not the

demander of it, or the author of it. You are in your authority in
the way that you may claim, but the response that you receive
is what you must be welcome to, to be in allowance with, or you
will not know what you need to know.

Now wisdom, we say, is a part of your inheritance. And you
mistake intelligence for wisdom and they are not the same
thing. Anybody can do the math who learns their times tables.
Anybody can do the construction that learns how to build
something with a hammer and a nail, but no one may know the
truth until he aligns to it. You may only know truth by aligning
to it. And we underline this, and say it a third time: *You may
only know truth by aligning to it.*

Now the fear that you have of truth is that it will lay waste
what you believe to be true. And when you see a forest on fire,
the first thing you want to do is put out the fire. Sometimes,
you know, the old growth needs to burn to allow for the new to
be born. And your attachment to what you have known is what
is being released through your interaction with us and the volume you hold in your hands.

The decision that you make to stand at the precipice and to
step off into the unknown is to welcome all the new possibilities that may be, but then you need your wisdom to claim them
in your worth. Just because something is there does not mean
you require it. Just because it may be seen does not mean you
must see it. And your wisdom will teach you. "I am wisdom"
will align you to wisdom if you are still enough to move into
the frequency of it and let it inform you. And let it inform you,

we will say, is the easiest way to understand this. You are all very used to controlling things, you know, so you believe when you are passive, or you are receptive, you are not doing anything, and you confuse this with action. To be in reception is an action. It is not inaction. It's a conscious choice to allow. If you allow this now, you will receive it now, and you will reap the benefits very quickly.

The authority you have, as the one who may claim her worth, gives her the right to claim other things as well. Do you understand this? If you can claim your authority as the one in worth, that entitles you to much more than you can imagine, and the gifts of the kingdom, we say, are yours for the claiming. But you must not do this in a cavalier way. You must not do this in fear. And you must not do this while scratching your head and wondering if you are worthy of it. Then you have to go back and read the book again until you understand you are.

Now, is everybody worthy of this? Absolutely, yes. At whatever level of consciousness they have attained, they are worthy. But they must know, and they must be in reception to this possibility in order for it to be made so in their response, in their frequency, and in their claim of dominion.

What you authorize, you see before you. We have said this many times. What you see before you, you are accepting as your own. Because it is there, you have agreed with it, it is there. Period. But what you may claim now in higher vibration is quite different from what you have known. It is a possibility of expression in higher consciousness as yourself in embodiment.

Now we must explain what this means, "embodiment." It means that you are anchored on this plane in a higher vibration than you have known, and that the expression of yourself that you are calling through you is of a magnitude and intent to claim you as itself. And the "itself" that is claiming you is your Christed Self, your Divine Self, the heritage that you know yourself through in your Son-ship of the Creator.

Now each of you are this no matter what and, as we have expressed before, there are different gradations of realization. In our first text, we expected you to witness your fellows and see the divinity in them so that you may rise above a frequency of judging your fellows and establish yourself in a new line of consciousness. When we ask you to do these things, we expect to see the results as you learn. You are tuning your radio, you know, to play the higher vibration.

Now, the theme of embodiment, while it is a grand theme, may not be quite what you think. Those of you who believe that you get to leave the life you have created and float away on a cloud are in for a grand disappointment. What you are becoming is you in your high potential, the potential that you can hold while manifested in form. It does not solve all your problems. It makes you accountable to your problems. But it gives you the tools to sort through them and the wisdom to re-create yourself, again and again, in accord with the new vision you are projecting outward.

Is it a lie that you can be this thing? Many of you are asking this already. Of course it is not. It is a potential. And when something is a potential, it is a possibility. And as we have explained earlier, when something is possible, it may be. In fact, what we are giving you is the system to attain a new level of your experience of yourself in your divinity while you have this experience here on this plane. And we do this for the benefit of all.

When we speak about the chapter of "The Kingdom" that we will come to shortly, we will address what it means on a planetary level for people to be in high vibration. But we will ask you, for now, to trust the process we are engaging you in. When we offer you wisdom, "I am wisdom, I am aligning to wisdom," and you go into reception as the wise one, you may claim your own information and operate in your own authority, which is exactly where we want you.

We do not want your authority. We have enough to handle with Paul some days. We are pleased for your presence and we are available to you, yes. But we are teachers and, as we have expressed, a good teacher wants his students to succeed. There is nothing in this text that we have expressed so far that will limit you in any way.

Now Paul is already asking, "Are they going to be frustrated? Are they going to be trying to align to wisdom and feel like they are banging their noggin against a wall?" Perhaps they may, it's an experience that they may choose. But it is not a requirement for knowing. You have all invested such expression in the path of struggle—that nothing is meritful unless it is hard won—that you cannot realize that wisdom is free. Wisdom is an inheritance. It may be called. There is universal wisdom that is all around you that may be tuned in to like a radio. When you align to your own wisdom, you are aligning to yourself as a conduit for wisdom so you may be expressed in wisdom.

When you are reactive, when you are frightened, when you are angry, you are never in your wisdom. You are operating in low vibration and you must attend to that so that you can go forward in a higher way.

Is wisdom available at a low vibration? Of course. But it is unlikely you will hear it, or know it, because you are being precluded by the lower thought-forms that you are engaged with. And that is always the temptation of the one who goes upward, you know, that you will be caught in a struggle of lower vibration that you have attended to for so long that you believe it must still be there.

If you can imagine rising up through a thunderstorm on the way to the sun that is above the clouds, you may not know the sun is there while you are struggling within the rain and the wind that is pummeling you. You do see what is above you, and you become so invested in fighting the storm that you believe that no sun can shine upon you again. That is what has happened to Paul some days, and it happens to all students as they elevate their vibration. There are times when you are challenged by what you have known, what you have been expressed through, what you have believed to be true, and there are times when you are not. There is growth in all stages, you know. But much of it means you must pay attention to your consciousness, and your consciousness, we say, is who you are in conscious thought and vibration.

You allow this, you know. You all allow your vibration to go up and down, and while you do that, you have different experiences of yourself. The lives that you will live soon, as you align to the high consciousness, the wisdom that is available to you will be significantly different, because you will no longer want to invest in the history you have ascribed yourselves to.

Now, what does it mean to be wise? It means to know. It also means to be humble. It does not mean you are the sole authority. It means you are receptive to wisdom, aligned to wisdom in consciousness, in accord with wisdom. It does not mean you are smart or that you know everything. The moment you think you know everything, you must know that you are being deceived.

If you look at a woman on the street and you ascribe a history to her based on her facial appearance, on her hair, and what she carries with her, you will most certainly be wrong. The first level of identification is always superficial, and most of you stop right where you start. Until you can look at a human being and see the infinite purpose behind them—"*I know who you are, I know what you are, I know how you serve*"—you will be in limitation and, you must know, there is always more to learn. So humility in the face of knowledge becomes quite important. The moment you seal a jar, nothing more may be put in it. You are the jar. If you put your lid on too quickly, you will not realize what may be known.

Now, we are asking you today to transcribe a lesson on wisdom that follows the chapter on the precipice. And we will see "The Precipice" as the introduction to the second section of this book. The new book we are speaking of is about being in your authority in wisdom and conscious sight: what you see before you and what you claim in your worth, in your visual sense, and in your identity. So we are looking at this as a second section of a book that will be written in several parts.

Now we are pleased for this, and the structure that is appearing before us will be of more benefit to the student of this text as she may attend to herself in different ways, in different stages, as she attends to the work on the page. We asked you earlier in this chapter to decide something new. To decide something new means what you may know. "Am I allowed to know?" Yes or no. And you must ask yourself this now. As you ask yourself this, we want you to prepare yourself to receive a response.

Now move into your own vibration, please, and align to your own vibration in the following words: *"I know who I am. I know what I am. I know how I serve."* And set this intention:

> "I am now aligning to my own knowing, my wisdom, and
> my inheritance."

And allow yourself to receive.

How you receive will be different and will be in accordance with what you can hold. You all have energy fields, you see, that are receptors, and how one man knows in his feelings may be different than another man knows in his body. How one man sees with his eyes will be different than one woman sees with her mind. One may feel, one may see, one may know in the body. So you must be prepared to learn what your receiver says, your receiver being the vehicle that you stand in, the body and the energy field that you are expressed through. So you ask your question, you move into your knowing, "I am wisdom, I am in my wisdom," and you go into alignment with that frequency to allow yourself to receive. Period.

Now, we will end this chapter shortly, but we will offer you this: The requirements of the times that you are in are that you each become your own authority for the higher good of all. This does not mean that you know more than the one beside you. It simply means that you move into your own knowing so that you may be of benefit to others. You are never the decider of another's fate. You never override their free will. You simply allow them to be in their own knowing.

When you are in your wisdom, you will be taught *by* wisdom as your inheritance unfolds before you:

"I am in my wisdom. I am taught by my wisdom. I will not be confused by information I have adhered to in my history to give me the answers to my questions today. I will be aligned to a new possibility, a new way of being expressed as the one who knows herself, himself, as wise."

We thank you all for your presence today and we will stop now. We would like to resume quickly. Not today, but soon. God bless you each. Good night. Stop now, please.

Day Eleven

We teach as we can. And the authority we have to be teachers is what we will address first. When one is a teacher, one has a responsibility to the student. And the responsibility we hold for each of you who reads this text is that we will engage with you as you stand before us as the one in willingness, who may learn, who may discover, who may reveal to himself, to herself, the wisdom that she has inherently. "Inherently" means within. We must tell you this, as we continue our chapter on wisdom, that we are not imparting something to you that is not yours already, but revealing to you what you have within you so that you may call upon your own resources, as you require.

You each know yourselves through those things around you, through those things that you have discovered, decided upon, accepted as true. You have revealed to yourself your lives thus far and you accept what you have created as what is there. The offering we give you now is to lift you up to a higher vantage point so that your perceptions may change. When you stand on the branch of a tree and you look at the horizon, the vision before you will be what you call to you from that height. When you stand upon a mountain and you call to you the view from that mountaintop, you are in that perspective and in that command of that level of perception.

Now, the requirements we have for you today are to lift the self to a higher level of perspective so that what you know is in accord with a higher way of being. There is nothing that you know now in your being, in your life, in your creation, that you have not accepted. Knowing and acceptance work concurrently. You cannot know something and not accept it; those things are in tandem. So the things that you adhere to, that you accept as true and know, are already in your purview. They are part of your landscape. You see them from the vision you hold and you have gone into accord with them.

Where we take you next is higher, to a lifting of your own mind to see what is before you from a new vision, a new way of perceiving, so that you may call to you the new knowing that is available from that height. Now height, we speak of as a metaphor for your own vibration, the conscious emanation of your field, the congruence that you hold with truth. And as you lift in this intention:

"On this day I choose to lift my mind, to lift my expression, to lift my availability to a higher level of knowing. I will claim the benefit of this choice. I accept my willingness to accept the teachings that are available to me at this new place, and I align my energy field to all that is required to sustain me at this new level of being. I am Word through this intention. Word I am Word."

what you are doing, in fact, is making a decision to realign your frequency beyond the boundaries you have created for yourself to a higher vision of what can be. And it is only from that perspective that you may have a new experience of yourself in perception.

Now you perceive everything. You see the cats and dogs, you see the fish, the people, the houses, whatever is before you. And you hold within your own knowing ways of identifying these things based on cultural heritage, the names you have been given to call things, and the acceptance you have given yourself of what is true and what is not. You don't tell a ten-year-old that a giraffe is a poodle. The ten-year-old will correct you very quickly. But what happens when there is a new creation? Something that has not yet been named that would enter into the field? How do you identify it? How do you accept it as true? When you have a new ideal, a new thought, a new possibility that has not yet been claimed or made manifest in form, you idealize the possibility—"There may be great things in the ethers that I do not know yet"—but you do not align to them as a reality because you do not have the tools and the ability to claim them.

When you do not know a math problem, the numbers on the page may float before you like a kind of gibberish. If you do not know a language and you are offered a book in the language, you will put it aside because you cannot understand the words on the page. This does not mean that the equation does not add up, or that the words on the page that have not been translated for you are not glorious and wonderful. They may well be, but because you cannot attend to them through your perception, you will never know unless you learn the new language, you learn how to add, the multiplication tables, and division to figure out the equation on the page.

Now, when we offer you this, very simply we are saying that these new ideas that we are offering you, that seem to be there above you somehow, are, in fact, possible but you cannot attend to them in fullness with the level of perception that you have held to this date. If you held the level of perception that would help you understand this, to call this into your being, to know it as so, we promise you this: You would have done it already. So what we are responsible for now, as your teachers, are lifting you to a new vantage point where this new understanding is possible, where the limitations you have used to keep yourself at bay no longer serve you and you move beyond them to a new acceptance of what is there always. And we say this with emphasis, *what is there always.*

As we lift you to a higher vantage point in your knowing, in your awareness, you are not discovering what has not been there, you are accepting what is there already. When an explorer went off in a boat and discovered a continent, he discovered what had been there always, but was misperceived, was thought to be illusory, legendary, but not fact. Our responsibility now, as you allow us, is to re-create your consciousness in accordance with the Word, in accordance with the Divine Self that you are, so that what you claim, what you perceive, is in alignment with this truth. The decisions you make from this level of awareness must be very different from what you have made in lower vibration, for the simple reason that you see things differently, you understand them differently, and you attend to the needs of the self and others from this perspective in a different way.

Now, conscious choice is always present and, as you have understood, when you lift your vibration to a higher level, you are the one accountable to it. If you wish to go down, you may go down, you may have that expression. But understand that when you have been high and in accordance with high vibration, you have one experience of your worth and the worth of everybody else, and when you go down, you have a very different one, and at each stage of consciousness you create things. The creations that you make in low vibration, in fear, in worry, in disregard of others' well-being, have repercussions, and you must attend to those repercussions in conscious ways.

We do not have the authority to take away your difficulties. We do have the authority to teach you how to attend to them. And the alignment that we are offering you now, to a higher vibration, a higher way of seeing, will do much of the work for you provided you set the intention to hold your vibration, and your awareness of the worth of your fellows, and the self in truth, in high and wise acknowledgment in the inherent divine within all. As you make this choice, you give yourself an anchor that you may hold to when you are tempted by lower vibration, by conscious choice that would bring you back down, by old patterns of fear, or negation of worth. When you still have a hand on the anchor, you have a hand on your own choice and, as we have said earlier, maintaining your vibration will always be your responsibility.

Now Paul is interrupting. "It is too hard. I can't get through a day without getting angry or being worried or projecting my fate in some uncomfortable way." You must understand, each of you, that so much of what you attend to is habit. This is habit, and a habit can be broken if you attend to it. If you have always gone to work left, right, and left, down the same road every day for many years, the impulse is to do the same regardless of the new path that has been laid for you. And the new path, we are telling you, is a much lighter path. It's a much more wonderful path. But so often, you revert to what the known has been, because you are challenged by the prospect of change, that it may not be what you want, what you seek, what you thought you were going to get when you made the choice to go on the journey.

Now, this is worthy of some discussion. You each decide, on an unconscious level, what it might be like to be in accord with higher wisdom, with higher vibration, with new choice, and the moment those choices don't adhere to the pictures that you have created, the temptation is to throw the book out the window, to decide that this is not a good path, or that the recommendations we offer you are too difficult to truly live by. And as you choose those things, you then make them so. You always get what you expect, in one form or another.

Now, when we tell you that the path before you may not be what you expect, we are simply telling you that it may not adhere to the promises you have made to yourself about what a life should look like. "Because I am now spiritual, my needs will all be met effortlessly, I will love my neighbor, I will see the beauty in everyone, and I will have to attend only to my own thoughts." Well, that is all well and good. But you do not arrive to a place of enlightenment without encountering those parts of you that would keep you in abeyance, that would keep you in the darkness. And we promise you this: There is no one who goes on this road who does not encounter herself, in all her fear, all her creations, and must come to the understanding that she is still loved. The aspect of you—and there are several aspects of you that would deny the darkness—will call you forward, and the aspects of you that would fear the light will keep you, as they can, in shadow.

Now, as we work with you, we pave the road. We pave the road for you so that your steps may be clear, so that you may not be alone, so that you may have a map of some kind, to show you where you go next. In our authority, we have offered you this through this trilogy of texts. The text that you hold now, in many ways, is the most ambitious of all of our three, because the transformations that you may be attended to through this, by this experience, will be lifelong and for the usherance of the new Word in all men.

As each one of you encounters yourself, accepts yourself, embraces what you have known and releases those things you no longer need to carry with you on your journey, you move into a kind of liberation of the soul. The personality, who has decided for so long what things must look like, how the path should unfold to conform to some ideal that somebody else once said was so, will be moved into proper alignment. And the withstanding of this, we say, in true recognition of the Divine Self as the aspect of you that has been born again, born anew, born through your expression, is what will heal others.

Now when we speak of healing others, you must understand that we are not giving you a ticket, an authorship to go about your business as a healer. So many of you run for your certificates, for those things that will tell you that you are allowed. In this case, the being that you are, expressed as you are, is the healing factor. The very presence of your being, in this alignment that we are offering you, is what will attend to the needs of others. So the obligation you have to them will be revealed to you by your own true self, but perhaps not in the way that you would think of now.

There are many ways to doctor someone. There is medicine and there is love. There is true recognition of worth, and there is the authority you bring as a conscious being who no longer aligns to a lower vibration. When you are encountered by somebody who holds low vibration, the opportunity that you have is to lift them to a new ideal, and this is done through your vibration, not necessarily through language or intentional action.

You may bless the one before you, and we recommend that

you do. "I am Word through the one I see before me" sets the intention that the vibration of the Word is within the other, and supporting them in their own evolution. "I know who you are, I know what you are, I know how you serve" claims them in truth and supports their vibration in aligning to their own Divine Self. The aspect of you that is their teacher will be brought forward in the way that is required, not as you would design it.

Now when we speak of designs, we are simply deciding to explain to you that when you design something in advance, you are usually designing something to attend to a frame that you have created previously, or you were taught would be there, should be there, must be there, if your life is to be right. "If my life is to be right, I will be married to the man of my dreams, doing wonderful work, making lots of money and surrounded by loving friends." That may be. That may be a false creation that you are using to frame a reality that may be much greater than the small mind would allow to be brought forward into manifestation.

You true soul's yearning, we say, is to be embodied in the Christ manifestation. That is the true soul's journey for all men. The times that you stand in now offer the opportunity for a rising, for an escalation of consciousness in a way that has never been possible on this plane. And the choice that each one of you makes to incarnate at this level supports all of mankind in doing the same.

We must say this one more time for the reader who becomes

frightened when we speak of the Christ manifested. The Christ, as we describe it, is simply the aspect of you, seeded by your Creator, that seeks realization *as* you. And the Divine Self you are, you must trust, knows his own path, knows her own path, and may know more than you know as you sit in your chair deciding what things should look like.

What does it mean to be in your wisdom at this new vantage point we speak of? It means to be in allowance, first and foremost, and we must express this to each of you who decides in advance that you need to know everything. To be in allowance and, as we have described earlier, to be in welcome, aligns you to the possibility of the wisdom that would be imparted to you, through you, in your inherent knowing. To decide in advance what an answer is may preclude the real answer from coming forward. So we offer you this exercise:

Take a moment now and simply be still and ask yourself a question that you know the answer to—"I know that my address is . . ." "I know the day of the week that this is . . ."—and then take a moment, and hear the answer come to you. Now take a pause and ask yourself a question that you do not know the answer to—"I know the reason I am . . ." "I am willing to know the reason I am . . ."—perhaps, if you wish to frame it as a question.

But when you go into a question, you must align to the possibility that the answer that comes will not be the convenient one, the one you had hoped for, the one your mother told you would be. So we offer you this: Ask yourself a question you do not know the answer to and be still and know. Now, knowing, we say, is not grabbing, it is not asking, it is receiving. You may claim your knowing in reception by allowing and aligning to it. "I am wisdom," as we told you, will align your vibration to the conscious knowing that may be available to you at any moment.

If you can imagine, right now, that there is a field surrounding this plane that holds all the information you could ever require, and attending to this information was not more difficult than aligning to it, you will begin to understand what we are teaching you. As you understand that there is a broadcast and you are the radio, you will begin to understand that the channels on the radio that you are may be refined to access information and your own wisdom at levels you have not encountered yet. It is available to you through acknowledgment and through welcome.

Now we will return to our initial subject of this day, which was the lifting of your own vibration to new perception, to what may be on the tree branch and visible from the mountaintop. And we would offer you this: The intention that you are setting now will work with you as you agree to it, and we underline *agree*. As we have said earlier, speaking words without a knowing, or a belief, or an acknowledgment of the truth in a statement will be words with no light. So we offer you this:

"On this day, I align myself to the next level of awareness that may be available to me in this incarnation. I set the intention that I am being attended to in this lifting so that I may see and perceive the information and the truth, the creations that are available to me at this level of sight. I agree to be supported in this alignment, and I offer myself to the guides who work with this text to support me in my own growth and well-being. I choose this of my own free will. As I lift my spirit, I lift my life. As I lift my life, all unfolds before me in perfect ways. I am Word through this intention. Word I am Word."

The lecture that we are giving you now is as much about responsibility as it is wisdom and perception, and we will echo this lecture, again and again, as we continue our teaching. Many of you wish to be taught, but you do not wish to do the homework. Many of you wish to receive information, but you do not want to attend to the possibilities that it offers you. Many of you wish to learn, but you do not wish to do. So we are supporting you each.

Paul is seeing the image of a ski lift. The skiers are all bundled up in their winter clothing and they are being carried up a mountain. And that is the appropriate image of today. We are carrying you up the mountain to the new view. You will see the new view, and you will decide for yourself what is before you.

We thank you for your presence today. We will resume tomorrow. Good night. Stop now, please.

SEVEN

THE DEMONSTRATION
OF LOVE

Day Twelve

We will teach. We will talk about love and responsibility and what you give to yourself when you believe you are worthy of love. The changes that you are undergoing now, as you engage with this text, are on two levels. Your own consciousness is acclimating to the information we offer you, and the vibratory field that you stand in is engaging with your changes and realigning itself to a new possibility.

As you expand your choices in the new worth you are claiming, you align to a new possibility: that the man that you are, that the woman that you are, is capable of great love. Now what does this mean? To be capable of great love means that you can have it to offer another, that you can be the vehicle for it, and the transmitter of the frequency of love.

Now the grounding that we are offering you now to bring you into accordance with love—"I know who I am, I know what I am, I know how I serve"—is an energetic shift in the frequency you hold that brings you into a foundation of material form that can be amplified as an expression of the divine. And the aspect of the divine that we are working with today is love incarnate, love as you, and the responsibility that you hold as the lover to all that you see before you.

Now Paul is getting in the way, "We have been taught love incarnate." Perhaps you have, but you are not demonstrating it. So we have to prepare a class in the demonstration of love. And we will call that the title of this chapter, "The Demonstration of Love."

Now when we speak of love, we encounter resistance from Paul, who still thinks that love is something that is unattainable, or an ideal that is a wonderful thing to speak of, but has no foundation in truth in his own experience. Of course, that is not so. And the first thing we have to do with each of you is define what you mean by love. When you say that you are in love, you are in a frequency, a divine frequency that will lift you to an expression of love in all that you encounter. When you are not in love, and not in accord with that vibration, your experience reflects that, and you offer yourself to a life without this alignment.

Now, as you align to love, to be expressed as love and, consequently, to demonstrate your consciousness in love, you are offering yourself to the world, and we will emphasize this, *you are offering yourself to the world.* You are not offering yourself to your best friend, or the person you always say hello to in what you would claim to be a loving way. You are offering yourself to the world as an energized aspect with the Creator in accord with love.

Now, the frequency that you hold today has been prepared for this work. And we will express this again: The frequency you hold today has been prepared for this work by your prior engagement with the work we have gifted you with thus far. So as you claim your worth, "I know who I am, what I am, how I serve," and you honor it, you claim the possibility that you may move into accord with divine love as your expression.

Now the responsibility you each hold is to realize, once and for all, that love is not a personality construct, nor is it special, to be handed to the special. It is the action of the Creator, working as and through you, in His own dominion, honoring all that He sees before him as a creation worthy of love.

Now, what is not worthy of love? If you ask yourself this, "What is not worthy of love?" you will discover very quickly the things that you put outside of God. And what you put outside of God you give great power to, because those very things you put outside of God keep you outside of God in your experience. Do you understand this? When you decide that someone is not worthy of the kingdom, you have decided that you are with them on the rock you place them on in isolation. You call yourself to that very thing you wish to not be expressed as, through your judgment and your fear.

So the first thing we will do with you now is make a decision that there will be nothing outside of God and, consequently, there will be nothing outside of God's love. Nothing you can imagine, nothing you have endured, nothing you have believed to be bad can be outside of God's love, because God is all things, expressing in different ways. And as you align to this new possibility, you can move in accord with the frequency of love in a new way.

If you wish now, take a piece of paper and write a list of all the things that you would keep outside of God, that you feel too good for, that you blame for this or that, that can never be forgiven or condoned. When you make this list, please ask yourself why you believe the things you do, who taught you these things, and why you create from them.

When you live in a culture that abandons their young because they have no parents or they are the wrong sex, you are operating from a fundamental wrong-mindedness, and there are cultures, indeed, that would perpetuate that behavior. Because it has been perpetuated does not make it a real thing, a true thing. It is a misalignment of value that many have accepted to be so. In your culture, you have many things that you decide cannot be of God. And those things that you claim outside of God are, in many ways, your master. Because as you adhere to the belief that they cannot be in union with the divine, that they cannot be accepted in the divine, in love and in the vibration of love, you keep yourself from it as well.

Now, this is not a revolutionary teaching, but it is what keeps many of you on the side of the road while the parade walks by. And you sit there in a kind of self-satisfaction that you are right to hold your beliefs and if others don't, they may go on their way.

We will tell you this: Where they are going, without the judgment that they hold, is to a higher place and you are welcome to join them, but not until you realize that love, as we say, is not exclusive, is not for the special, nor is it for those you decide to be in love with. And we say "in love" not in a romantic sense, but in the true sense. As you are the expression of love, you are the conduit of love. Love flows through you and expresses itself to all you see before you. Now here we go:

> "On this day I choose to realign my vibration to the highest expression of love that I may hold. And I give myself permission to release any and all judgment of what cannot be loved, who cannot be loved, and I allow myself to accept my former choices as born in what I believed. And I relinquish the beliefs that have held me in abeyance so I may rise to a new understanding of love, and express as love in truth and knowing. As I say this, I know it is true. I am claiming my power back from any expressions of value that are not in alignment to love, and I give myself permission to reclaim myself as the expression of God in love that I am intended to be. I am Word through this intention. Word I am Word."

Paul is feeling his energy shift as he claims this, and we expect that you will feel the same as you align to this decree. To be in your honor is to be in your integrity. You do not denounce another from a place of judgment. You do not denounce another from a place of self-righteousness. You have no right, we will say, to hold yourself above another in any way and, as you do, you release yourself from the promise of being demonstrated as love.

Now when you stand in your knowing, "I know who I am, I know what I am, I know how I serve," you have created a path. And as we walk you down this path, we want you to see the creations you have made that guide the way on each side. What do I claim here? Where am I not in my worth there? These are the sights that show themselves as you walk forward, and they are never shown to you to keep you in place, but as an opportunity to grow and move forward in your awareness of your worth.

When you see something on the path that does not feel in congruence with the vibration of love, when you fear it, when you demand it gone, we will ask you to do this: Claim it in the Word. "I am Word through this thing I see before me." "I am Word through this old belief system." "I am Word through this fear I see that I believe will overtake me." As you claim the power of the Word in all of these manifestations on the path, you align them to the Christ. They become reborn, as do you, and they become your invitation to continue forward.

How you choose to attend to each obstacle that presents itself on the road will be in operation of your consciousness at the level you have attained. The day when you no longer act upon an old fear, the day that you realize that your neighbor is your love and not your enemy, the day that you decide that the only thing that hampers you on the road before you is the illusion of separation, you create a new way of being yourself as love.

Now the demonstration of love as you is a frequency that you are in alignment with. The alignment of this frequency is something that may be expressed as you in ways that you may know. "I am Word through my body" sets the intention that the physical body is in accordance with the Word. "I am love through my body" sets the intention that the vibration of love is in accord with you and may be expressed in your physical self. "I am love through my vibration," "I am love through my knowing of myself as Word," we have claimed will align your physical body, your vibrational field, and your identity to the frequency of love.

As you stand in this vibration, you must demonstrate it, and to do this you need to give yourself permission to dismantle those creations that have been used to stand in the way of your expression as love. Now, why would anyone create an expression to oppose the vibration of love? Why would you build a house and shield yourself from love? Well, you do this because you have been taught that it is not safe to allow others close. You have done this because you have had experiences that proved that to be true. And as you create a wall between yourself and your fellows, you preclude them from expressing themselves as love to you, and vice versa. As you realize what we teach, and by realize we mean "know in your expression," you may understand that the invitation of others to be loved, to be seen in love, will amplify your consciousness in ways that you may know and demonstrate.

As you walk on your path today, we would like you to take a moment to see each one before you, each one you pass on the street, in a store, in a library, in a park, as worthy of the love of the Creator regardless of what they have done, believe themselves to have done, or known. As you do this, you impart yourself the same gift, "I am worthy of love." And as you demonstrate the consciousness of love—"I see all before me in love, I am in alignment to love, and I see love in all things before me"—you become an expression of love. The actions that you take are in accord with love and love becomes your vibration.

Now the song that you sing as love in your consciousness is magnificent and will be heard by many on the inner planes. The love that you express and demonstrate in your life will be witnessed by many, in the ways that are appropriate to know, and you will be gifted in response because love is its own reward.

Now Paul is asking, "Is it so easy, really, to be love? To be expressed as love? Am I allowed to do this, or will I be disappointed by my walk, by my witnessing?" We will offer you this, Paul. You have as much right to love as any man, and there is no man who is unworthy of the gift of the Creator.

The exercise that we are giving you is to show you that this is so in your expression. If you are walking down the path and you see someone you would withhold love from, why are you frightened? What was your teaching and how does it benefit you? Is it worth holding on to if it keeps you a prisoner, if it keeps you from love? If it is not, and we will tell you it never is, you may thank the old expression. It was created at a time when it was necessary for you, or imparted to you as a way to keep you safe in a way that is no longer needed today, and you accept the thing before you in love, as having a right to be loved. That is the first step.

When you believe that everything has a right to be loved, from the lowest creature to the highest, from the imbecile to the sage, from the young man to the old, you will witness yourself in love, and the sight that you behold will be the sight of the Christ. And we will say this again: *The sight that you behold will be of the eyes of Christ.* When you witness all before you with the eyes of Christ, which is in love, the mastery that you will hold will carry you to your next teaching. And we will say this many times: As you learn a lesson, as you create yourself anew, you offer yourself the possibility of your next steps forward and the path is laid for you to progress.

The demonstration of love as you is not a challenge. It is a much easier way to be in the world than you can even imagine. But you lack practice, and you lack faith. You lack the belief that you know that you will be safe if you are the lover. Now, to be the lover does not demand anything in return from anybody. And if you think that love demands return, you are playing games with yourself. Love is its own reward, and love demonstrates itself as you in ways that you will see and know. But the gift that you are given by love, by love, by love is the gift of the kingdom.

When you see with the eyes of the Christ, something begins to happen, which is the creation of heaven on earth in a way that you may perceive. Paul is asking, is this different than seeing the perfection in all men? Yes, it is, in a way. When you walk down the street and you witness everyone in their perfect place, their perfect sense of self, given the level of awareness that they have attained at this time, you are perceiving divine order. And you are perceiving the perception of truth in the balance and evolution of all things. When you move into the conscious intention to love, you vibrate in a higher way to embrace and to lift. When you are judging, you do not love. When you are frightened, you do not love. When you see the one before you in their worth and as worthy of love, you heal. You gift them, and, by gifting them, you gift yourself.

We are the teachers here. And we are saying this because Paul is asking if we can stop soon—there is a pretty day outside. We will say there is a pretty day outside every day you see love. Every day you witness the divine in the creations before you. Every day that you decide that you are worthy of seeing these things, they will be brought to you.

The decision that you make that life is hard, that there is no love for you, that mankind cannot be transformed keeps you in static space. It keeps you from moving forward to the possibility of great change born in worth. So the dismantling of those things has been the work we have been attending to. As you dismantle a structure, you create the possibility of a new foundation, and in this case the new man, the new woman that is born, that is ascended, that is transformed by her own worth is the product of the effort we are all intending on your behalf.

The requirements for change, we say, are very simple:

"I am making the choice to change. I am choosing to realign my vibration to love. And I am giving myself permission to relinquish those things that I have held dear that may no longer serve me on the path that has been laid before me."

Those are the choices you make. As you make each choice, you are attended to in the level of worth that you have aligned to. "That you have aligned to" is key. When one of you has a long road ahead of you to claim the simplest sense of self-worth, you will be led there well. But you cannot claim what you cannot hold. And as we teach you to hold in your vibratory frequency the level of awareness and justice and truth that may be manifested as you, the bells ring and your resonance, we say, is what claims you and your fellows in divine love.

The song that we sing today, "It is a perfect day, it is a new day, all things are possible whether or not they may be seen," is for you to accept as so regardless of what you may think. The thoughts that you hold about what may be and what may not are what tether you to what may be and what may not. So the decision you make now, to relinquish those things that would obscure love and consequently stop you from your own level of knowing of yourself as love, is your expression and your teaching for this day.

"On this day I choose to know my worth in love. On this day I decide to know the worth of all in love, regardless of

my previous perceptions of them. On this day I know that
all are worthy of love, and my sight, my expression affirms
this every moment of my waking day. I know that this is so.
I am Word through this intention. Word I am Word."

We have a plan for you, you know. And it is a good one. But you
must attend to the teachings. As we leave you today, we will ask
you one more thing. Tell one human being in your life that you
love them, and align yourself to that as a frequency. When you
do this, you will reap a benefit. And then you will go out and
love the world.

We thank you for your attentions today. Good night. Stop
now, please.

Day Thirteen

We are responding to the needs of the reader now. Those of you
who decide that you are worthy of love will begin to have a
change in your expression. Those of you who decide you will
wait until it is safe to be loved will have a different experience.
Those of you that know yourselves as loved will change your
lives in the realization of your own providence, of your own
choice to be in emanation as love.

You are always choosing, you know. The choice to be in
love, to be responding as love, to be awakened as love, is here
for you to choose, but you must decide that it can be so. It can

be so, you know. There is no magic here. Those of you think we are embedding you with a magical ideal are in for a big surprise. What we are doing is awakening you to your own knowing, to your own worth, so that you may be in accord with love and with the benefits of love.

All of you have relationships, yes. You decide the people you call to you to bring you what you need in your evolution. Your relationships, we say, in many ways, are your greatest teachers because you can see how you invest your needs for others to be in response to you. How you decide they should act and claim their own worth. You value people, like it or not, on how they make you feel. "I feel good when I am with him, I will stay." "I do not feel good when I am with her, I will leave." You have an opportunity through this to know what you feel, but you also have an opportunity to learn who you are through the feelings you have and the experiences you call to you. You are the decider of this, in many ways, but you do not know it.

When you hold a frame before you—and a frame is what you choose to frame your experience—you always call something to you that will be expressed in accordance with the mandates, or the requirements, of that frame. You all decide what your frames are. How you claim a frame, in many ways, is born in your history, personally, collectively, and the history of your plane. "We must do this because this is who we are" is a claim of group identity. And a group identity, when it is claimed, becomes something that you all elect to go into agreement about. The frames that you hold individually are what we are attending to today in response to your own need to be the one in love.

When you are cherished by another, you are held in love. When you are being thoughtful to another, to their needs, to their requirements, you are responding from a place of love. But we will tell you this: The action of love is to reproduce itself out-pictured in your frequency. And you must hear us when we say these words: As you move into accord with love, you express love and love becomes your world. As long as love is predicated on emotion, or your response to be cherished, or getting your needs met in the way that you think you should, you will be in limitation as a conduit for love. Because the valve can close at any moment when you do not get what you need, when you do not experience yourself as cherished, or as a beloved.

The question, then, becomes how do you be love incarnate when you are not being gifted with what you want, what you think you should have, or what you were told you should receive? How do you be in love in the face of challenge, of others' behavior, of creations that challenge the foundation of what it means to be love? How do you love the one who killed your child? How do you love the one who betrayed you? How do you love the authority that persecuted you, or the system of governance that took your home and left you without anything?

These are real questions and we understand them. But the first thing you must know is that the action of love never steals, never lies, never blames, never harms. The action of love, and the action of love as you, is only to gift your expression as love.

When you tether love to an outcome that is born in your expectation, you will fail. "I will love her as long as she . . ." "I will love this as long as I . . ."—you fill in the blank for yourself. Those are precursors to shutting off the valve that would express you as love. Now, what you do in the face of challenge, when you are confronted with something that you believe cannot be loved, is to decide that there is a new possibility. And we underline this: *there is a new possibility.*

As you understand the name that you have been given, "I know who I am, I know what I am, I know how I serve," you claim your authority and thereby you claim your inheritance as the one in choice who may call the kingdom into being. The sacrifice that you make by doing this is fear, and all the things that you believe would keep you from loving another are born in fear. "He did this, he cannot be loved. I will be fearful if he is loved." "She is not allowed to be loved, look at what she has done, and the pain that she has caused. I will not love her." You seal yourself, then, in your own cave and you write on the walls, again and again, all the reasons why it is not safe to love.

Now, we do not tell you that love is something that you do other than be expressed. As you are expressed as love, the requirements of love are claimed by you, and you move into accord with what is required of you at that level of expression. Condemnation of another only calls condemnation to you. But how do you love the one who hurt your child, who broke your heart, who burned your house down or rendered you powerless when all you wanted was power? You forgive them, yes, but first and foremost you have to know who they are. And we will tell you this, like it or not, and many of you do not wish to hear this: They are as loved as you are by the divine and they are having their expression. As long as you know that they are worthy of love, you align to the possibility that you may be in that current and you may be in that expression.

The Divine Self that you are does not hold grudges. She does not want them, she knows what they incur. The master that you are in your higher knowing believes everybody to be in their worth regardless of what they have chosen. As you align to love, "I know who I am in love, what I am in love, how I serve in love," you claim them in the same way.

We want you now to see one before you that you keep outside of the light, that you shut away, that you blame, that you may hate, that you may claim is the reason for your pain or suffering. Put them before you and see them as they are: an aspect of the divine seeking its own expression, divine love incarnate. And we say these words to them as we see them before us:

"I know who you are, I know what you are, I know how you serve."

And as you witness them as they truly are, an aspect of God bound in their fear or in their choice to behave in one way or another, you begin to relinquish the fear that you have held. Once the fear is relinquished, the action of the divine will come through to regulate the aspect of you that wishes to blame, seeks to return to what you have known, seeks to condemn. The aspect of you that is witnessing the aspect of the divine in them is the aspect of you coming into manifestation as you attend to our words. We are only asking you this: Forgive yourself for the need to punish another to feel that you are safe, to feel that you are right. Forgive yourself for the need to be expressed in rage or condemnation so you may greet the one before you in love.

Now understand this, please. When you love another, you hold them in their worth. That is what you do, and you hold them in their worth unconditionally. There is nothing possible for any man to do, for any woman to do, to make them unlovable by God, but they do not know this. They shut themselves away, and you heal that by seeing them in their worth. If you condemn them, if you roll the stone in front of your own cave to block out the light, you harm yourself.

Now we will tell you something. You don't have to like them. You don't have to dine with them. You don't have to sing their praises as a loving soul. You need to honor them in their worth, and that is all the difference.

The suffering of man at the hands of his fellows is tragic. You do not hurt what you love. You do not sing the song of love that we sing to you to someone you condemn. You want your condemnation, that is the road you will travel. And we will tell you this: This is the road you have traveled as a people, and we intervene with our message now so that you may realign your purpose to your intended purpose, to incarnate as love for the benefit of all. And we say "all" with the meaning that it is inclusive of the one you wish to burn in hell. Do you understand?

Now we will speak of hell. It is a creation of consciousness. And like any creation of consciousness, it can be made manifest as you attend to it. What is war if it is not hell? And what is hell as war but a creation of mankind? If you wish to change yourself, stop harming yourself. When you stop harming yourself, you will not harm your fellows, and we promise you this. There was a time, you know, when the outcast was hung in the town square. Now you go to the movies and watch it pretend before you, watch the hanging on the screen and feel solvent. In fact, what you are doing is the same. You are seeing the one before you in their penance, and you feel justified when the villain is killed at the end of the tale. You feel that the world has been restored. Never once do you think that the villain might be in requirement of divine love.

Now if you did the exercise that we taught you, and you witnessed the one before you in their worth that you would shut away, you have given yourself an opportunity to be liberated from the very thing that tethers you to your fear, from the very thing that keeps you up at night in worry or in shame. The relationships you hold, like it or not, are reflections of your consciousness and your own sense of self. When you are not valued by another, you must discover where you do not value yourself, or why you believe that this is appropriate behavior, for you to be mistreated, or hurt.

As you claim your power back, as you align to a new possibility of choice, "I am in my choice to know my worth," we promise you this: The relationships that you hold must be transformed in regard to the claim you have made.

When you write a story, you imagine an ending. You claim something to be so. You may not know how you arrive to the ending, but you know you will go where you intend to. Now we say this: When you decide "I know who I am in love, I know what I am in love, I know how I serve in love," you claim your power as the vehicle of love and it is expressed as you, and we honor you by supporting the vibration in all you claim as the new reflection of your worth. It cannot be otherwise, you know.

The destiny of man, we say, is to be in alignment of his awareness of his Divine Self and in authorship of his expression in mastery. To be in mastery means you know who you are, you know what you are, you know how you serve, and it is so. And we underline this, *it is so.*

Now the honoring you do of your process as you engage with our words is to realign the vibrations that you have held to the new possibility so that you may liberate yourself from the structures and creations, if you wish, the frames that you have held and claimed as yourself. You always claim yourself, you know. You always will. The honoring that we give to you, each of you—no one is excluded—is that we know your merit, even when you do not. We see your beauty even when you do not. We recognize your divinity even when you do not and even when you refuse it.

The divinity that you hold, the Christ within you if you wish, the divine spark if you like, the Shekinah if you wish, the Holy Spirit if you want—you can call it what you like—the aspect of the Creator as you that has come to be sung knows the words to the song already.

We do not address the Divine Self. She knows her business better than you do. We do address the personality who would claim herself in retribution, who needs to realign her belief in what may be so, so that the heart may sing its new song.

Now, we love you each, and we do not say this lightly. We do not speak of affection, or Valentine's Day cards. We speak of love as the aspect of the Creator we recognize in truth. We know who you are and we love you as you are, and you do not change because we tell you to. We love you regardless. We only offer and extend a hand to take you over the gulf that you have created between you and your own divinity.

As you stand on the new shore, you welcome others to you. Because you have been embodied, you vibrate as love and you sing the song of love and you see each one before you as she truly is: a miracle having an expression of herself in this insane and magical and perfect school you have all agreed to attend.

Now, honoring this and the agreement to be here with your fellows in your relationships and your encounters as ones who learn, gives you each permission to be where you are at each stage of your learning. You cannot expect the seven-year-old to do college math. You cannot expect the child without the map to find her way home. We are offering you a map right now to your own self, to your own way to you, so that you may welcome your fellows.

Now we ask you this: As we continue our text, we understand that there are questions that emerge from the reader. If you would, in your mind, set the intention now that these questions are being responded to by us, as you require them. We will attend to you as you are, where you are, and incorporate as we can in the dictation we give through Paul.

Now, you may ask how this is done. The membrane that you know as time is permeable. You are traveling all over the place in your expression without your body, as your consciousness, all the time. The difference is that we know who you are and we may attend to you where you are and continue our teaching as needed.

We will take a pause now, and we will resume tomorrow. We congratulate you both for your attendance today and we will offer the reader this: We are with you. Good night and thank you. Stop now, please.

Day Fourteen

We respect you each as you decide, as you claim, as you will, as you choose, as you give, as you respond to your own needs. We respect you as you act, as you make news, as you call things to you, as you express yourselves in all ways.

Now today we will ask you one thing: Do you respect the

self that you are? Do you align to respect as an attitude, as a way of being in the world? If you do not, we will teach you. And if you do, you will teach yourselves how to be expressed as the one who is respected in a whole new way.

We talk about divinity very often. The aspect of the Creator within you that may be manifested as you is the Divine Self, seeking expression and being amplified through your engagement with us and the writings that we offer you. The Divine Self that you know as yourself is still precluded from full expression by several things: Your belief that it cannot be so, your fear of what it means to be realized, and the responsibility that you hold in your mind if you are activated and realized at a higher level of awareness. The fear that it cannot be so is what we will attend to first.

You are all in manifestation in one way or another, you all have creations you see before you, and you may all agree that you are in inheritance of those things that were created by you and that you have accepted from others. It is everything that you see before you. At this time, we are simply saying to you that the new alignment you are being offered will claim you in a new vibration that must be in accord with a new way of living a life. If you can accept this much, you have already engaged in an escalation of your own consciousness that will benefit you and call to you those things that you must know to realize this, to know this, to claim it as true.

You are the one in charge of your identity. We have said this many times, and we remind you once again: You are who you say you are. When you claim your divinity and you design an out-picturing, a life to be expressed in accord with that, the landscape is changed and everything that you see must move into accord with it. The fear that it cannot be so is the fear of climbing higher. It is the fear of being seen at the top of the tree by the ones below you who say, "Come down, come down, it is not safe to ascend."

We will tell you one thing: Ascension, we say, is a state of consciousness that accelerates you and attends to your vibration as you create things on this plane. So, consequently, the creations that you make from higher consciousness will align to you. Those things that adhere to lower vibration stop impacting you because you are not in alignment with them. Now, this is not magic. This is systematized.

As you each grow up, the expectations of the age you stand in are given to you. When you are old enough to leave your home, you find your own home, you supply your own food. This, in many ways, is no different. The vibration that you call to you will give you the need to know what you require at that level. The demonstration of this, we say, at each level of awareness, is something you may know, see before you, and call to you. Can it be so? Yes. It already is so. You are all demonstrating your consciousness wherever you stand. So imagine only that the arm is reaching higher to call you forward to your next incarnation as you stand in your own being.

The fear that it cannot be so, we say, is a way to keep you safe within the structures you have created thus far. It is a way to decide what you are allowed in a way that does not challenge what you have known. Can it be so? Yes. Will it be so? That is your choice. The designs that you hold, up until today, have been created to benefit you. They are the stepping-stones as you go forward, and they will lift you if you see them for what they are, simple structures that you have decided upon to give yourself this experience of alignment on this plane.

Now Paul is getting in the way, "Well, so what if it cannot be so, if it can be so, what is so today? What am I today, and what do I do next to remain in my alignment, to change my life, to call to me the next adventure of my consciousness?"

As you stand before yourselves today, you must make a decision. The demonstration of love and the responsibility of love as you must extend to all you see before you. And the respect that you hold for your true self must be known by you in a way that you can attend to. The fear of being respected by others, or the demand to be respected by others, has nothing to do with you. In fact, the only respect that you need is from yourself. And the respect that we attend to today, the vibration that you hold as respected, is what you give permission to align to.

Now the holding of a single vibration calls to you a single thing. The holding of a greater vibration calls to you a greater thing. The fear that you have of being demonstrated, in your majesty, as an aspect of God, demonstrates to all things that you hold outside of God. As we have taught you thus far, what you hold outside of God gives that mastery over you, because it is ruling you. What you give your response to in any day is what you give your attention to, and what you hold outside of God, you have aligned to, like it or not.

Now, how do you respect yourself? How do you give permission in your self-worth to accept yourself as the one worthy of the kingdom? We will ask you one thing: Why would you not be? If you would take a piece of paper now and write all the things you do not respect of others, you will see a reflection of yourself, like it or not, because these things that you write you are still in accord to, and you choose to align to.

Now we are not saying that people will do what you want, or behave in accordance with what you think they should, once you are changed. But we will tell you one thing: What you align to is an accurate reflection of yourself. The need to harm another corresponds directly with the need to harm the self. The need to judge another corresponds directly with the need to judge the self, and the demonstration of these things are what you claim as you, each and every day.

When you respect yourself in truth, when you decide you are worthy of love and can be respected in any way, you align to respect. And in the alignment of respect to the self, you align to the respect of all you see before you.

"Well, what if somebody is not respectable?" you may ask. What you choose to respect is in accord with what you have been taught. How you decide upon another is a direct reflection of your own history. We will tell you one thing: Anytime you look at another human being and you see them before you, you are calling your own history to them. You are perceiving them through a frame that you have held that idealizes some things, criticizes others, and makes assumptions based on what you see. "The man with the crumb on his beard does not take good care of himself." "The woman with too much makeup has an issue with how she looks." You assume these things and you may be right on a surface level, but you are out-picturing your own consciousness and thereby denying them the respect that they are due. This is no mystery. If you stand before a mirror and you see yourself, you see who you expect to see. You do not see the self as you are seen by others. You see the image before you and you align to what you think you are.

The hopeful choice for each of you is to realize right now that the one you see before you, the aspect of the Creator that you see before you, is infinite, has no crumb in the beard, does not require makeup, is who she is, is who he is, in a wonderful way. You must no longer assume anything. You must no longer decide in advance who and what you think you are. If you do, you lie, and we say "lie" because you are telling yourself an untruth every day you say that you are in limitation. You are not in limitation. You attend to limitation; you re-create limitation as conscious beings who have been told you are not allowed to align to truth.

Now, what happens when you ascend in consciousness? What is the vehicle of your expression asking from you? How do you attend to the needs of yourself at this level of incarnation?

They are fair questions, but you presume things. You presume that the answers will fit the reality that you have known thus far. In fact, they cannot. The reality that you have known thus far is predicated on your history and history, we say, is no longer meritful of a way of knowing the self. It is a condemnation of your present to think of yourself as your history, because the history that you impose in many ways is colored and formed by belief systems that you attended to prior to your awareness of your divinity and the divinity of everybody else. Do you understand this?

When you had a size shoe at age ten, it was, perhaps, very small. You do not go to the shoe store and ask for that same shoe. If you are acting on your history, what you will claim will not fit you. The same is true for identity. How do you honor yourself as you grow is a more pertinent question. How do you lift your vibration, when you decide for another what you are, and what you are not, that you honor, or dishonor in your way? How do you re-create yourself as the one who knows in the face of ignorance, in the face of what you have thought, that you now question to be true?

Now we ask you one thing: Have you decided yet that you are worthy of love? Have you made that decision yet? Do you allow the possibility that we respect you enough, that we care for you enough to support you in this opening? That we may hold you in esteem, in the regard that you deserve, so you may align to the possibility of love for your own highest good and for the good of all?

As you decide you can do this, the way is made for you. The path is clear and your experience, as we have told you, will be transformed. The identity that you know yourself through as your history is going to be disembarked from. Imagine it is a shore that you have known, and the courage that you need now is to align to the new hope that your embodiment, the demonstration and the responsibility of love that you hold, will be met at the journey's end.

We say yes now. As we say yes, we move into the vibration of yes, of permission, of allowance, and we ask you to do the same.

"I know myself in love. I know myself in esteem and I claim that I am worthy of love. I know who I am, I know what I am, I know how I serve. I am Word through this intention, Word I am Word."

We thank you each for your time today. We will continue our teaching soon. We will say that this is the end of the last chapter. As we move forward, we will continue to answer the questions that we raised today, and we will continue to work with you as you choose to be loved.

"I am Word through the ones I see before me. Word I am Word."

Thank you and good night. Stop now, please.

EIGHT

HOW YOU WITNESS

Day Fifteen

Now we want you each to know one thing: You are deciding
your fate every time you stand up and you claim your provenance over the things you see before you. "I am in charge of
this aspect of my life." "I am not in charge of that aspect of my
life." To decide what you can handle, what is yours to decide
over, will give you the direction you need to call your experience to you in ways that would benefit you. What is not your
purview is the will of another. And we will stress this: *You are
never in charge of the will of another.* The sanctity of individual
choice, the free will that you have been gifted with, is the issue
of the day. And who you know yourself as in your provenance,
in your jurisdiction, is what we will attend to.

Now the fears that you have of being in charge of your own
lives is significant. You do not want power because you are
frightened of it, you have been told you will not handle it well,
or you cannot hold it. In fact you can, in fact you have a right to

it, in fact your choice, every moment of every day regardless of what you think, is to stand in your power and, we will say, that includes when you defer your authority to another. That is your choice as well.

The dominion that you have been gifted with, individually and collectively, is the claim you agree to when you come into manifestation. There is no way around this. There is no easy route outside of your claim, which is why we emphasize in our teaching that you are the one in choice, again and again and again. Now when you have questions about the implications of this on your world, we will address them as we can. But the first thing you need to understand is that the ridicule of the self—"I am not powerful enough to change the world," "I am not in authority enough to make a good difference"—is a lie you tell yourself, agree to, and create from.

Now if you are powerful, what does that mean? That does not mean you're an outlaw. That does not mean you abuse your power. In fact, the opposite is true. If you attend to our teachings, the first thing you will understand is that the escalation of your vibration incurs a responsibility. To hold your vibration in high regard requires you to do the same for everybody else. To believe that one person could misuse this information to create chaos assumes that that person is aware of their own vibration. You cannot create chaos from the Christ consciousness. How could that possibly be? But we will tell you this: Claiming mastery does regard existing structures, laws, attributes that you have agreed to, up for questioning.

Now we will tell you what this means. It does not mean you break the law, it means you understand who you are as the one in choice to adhere. Every time mankind makes a leap in his own awareness of his purview, there is resistance. And the resistance that you attend to with our teaching is that you cannot be who you say you are, that you are not allowed or, if you are, you cannot hold it, you will be crushed by the responsibility of choice that you are being given.

To assume these things assumes that you are carrying your old baggage with you, your little bag of tricks. "Well, I should be doing this or that." "It should be this way or that way." Imagine you are going to a hotel room in a fine hotel on the very top floor. You are not needing anything because all will be supplied to you. But you insist on carrying your old leather bag with the patches on it, and all the garbage you've accrued, up to this new fine room, because if it is not there you will not know who you are. And this is the teaching of history. The old leather bag was serviceable, but do you require it at the new level that you are attending to? You do not.

Now we will tell you one thing: History and information are not necessarily the same thing. Knowing how to tie your shoelaces is information. Being told that you are stupid when you did not get it right when you were four years old is your history. Do you understand the difference? What you do not need to carry in your ascension to the upper room are those things that you've accrued that want to tell you what the view should be looking like outside of the new windows. You assume to see what you think you should see. You perceive what you think you should, based on what you have known. If you are standing at a window and you see the Eiffel Tower, you say, "I must be in France, that is where the Eiffel Tower is." Perhaps it was moved. Perhaps it is a false structure. But you attend to what you see based on what you were taught.

Now, what is the vision from the high floor? That is the question you would ask. We will tell you what the answer is now. The view is unobscured by fear. That is the view from the high floor. The view is not a fearful view. It is a mastery. You see what is before you, you know what it is, and you are in agreement with truth. You do not judge from the view and, in fact, the view does not allow judgment. That was left on the lower floor. You cannot rise to the level we would take you to if you want to carry your judgment, the names you claimed for how things should be. What a waste it would be to travel to a new country where all the food is new and say, "Where is my cheeseburger? There must be a cheeseburger, that is what I know food to be." You dismiss the new offering and you go back to where you know how to get a cheeseburger.

Now, we are not saying that you cannot keep remnants of your world in your ascension. Imagine that from the high view, everything that you see before you and that you have known is still there, because in fact it is. But how you perceive it has changed. The vision is different, the vantage point has changed and your understanding, we will say, of what you see before you has altered in accordance with the new level of consciousness that you have agreed to.

Can anybody misuse this information in our text? Anybody can do anything they like. But if they are attending to the teachings, and not attempting to distort them to fit a paradigm that would serve the ego, they are attended to by us. We shepherd the students through the classes that we teach, and we see the ones who need to, perhaps, take the test again before they may go to the next level. Now, that is not a punitive statement. Why would we let somebody behind the wheel of a car who will crash it? We want to keep you safe, and in your awareness of your worth so that you may learn. We want you in your worth so you may see the worth in your fellows. We want you to decide for yourselves because if you are not deciding for yourself, you are giving your power to others.

Now what does it mean to give your power to another? To let them tell you who they are and for you to go into agreement with them. "I am the one in charge," and you say, "Okay, you must be," and there goes your power. When somebody says they are the one in charge, you may understand that they are fulfilling a role. The one behind the cash register at the market has been designated to take the money and, in that instance, she is in charge of the money. The job that you keep may tell you what hours to attend to your work at and, in fact, yes, they are in charge of dictating the schedule, but these people only have the power that you offer them. The belief that they have more power than you is something that you have agreed upon, moved into accordance with, and manifested, and that is the collective choice.

When somebody else tells you who you are, "I know who you are, I know what you are, I know how you serve," they are witnessing you in your worth. When you are witnessed in your worth, you may go into agreement with your worth and, consequently, serve from that place. The identity that you give yourself, "I know who I am, what I am, how I serve," supports you in grounding this knowing as, underline *as,* your expression.

Now, decisions are made in fear, decisions are made in ignorance, decisions are made when they are brought to you to make. How you attend to your decisions and from what aspect of consciousness is an important thing to know. As you go into agreement with your worth, and your choices are made in your worth, you dictate the trajectory of your future.

Now, what does it mean to be in your worth in this way? It means that you know you are the one in choice. And that is really what it means: that you are the one in choice to agree, to decide, to bring to you what is offered, what may be gifted, what may be known. When you make a choice in ignorance, you do not know. When you make a choice because you think you are supposed to, you may be making a choice in your worth, or you may not. How do you know? We will tell you: You claim your power as the one who may know. And as you may know, you will know.

Now we say this: Because somebody asks you a question does not mean you have to give them an answer on the timetable they wish. You still are allowed process, you may go into your own conscious mind, you may go into your own discernment, you may go into what you have known, if you like, to see if the information you need is there to support you. When you move into your own knowing—and Paul is holding his heart as he says this, because your knowing, we will say, is in the heart center, and in the vibration you hold—you align. In the alignment of knowing, you may know.

When you are asked something and you do not know the answer, you may discover the answer in any way. Paul cannot add two and two without a calculator in front of him. He is not the person to ask about a theorem. Somebody else may well be. Just because the information exists in the world does not mean you are all responsible to know it. But there are things you do know: Am I worthy of this choice? Am I aligned to my worth in this action? Am acting in my fear? Am I in my provenance as the one who knows that she may choose? Am I in my limitation, believing that some things are not available to me? You will answer your own question and claim these words:

"I know who I am. I know what I am. I know how I serve. And I am claiming my knowing in this instance, in this situation, in this requirement. I am Word through this intention. Word I am Word."

What this does is align your vibration. "I have claimed that I am the one who knows," which gives you permission on a higher level to realign yourself to the requirements, or the information you seek.

Now when you ask yourself a question and you hear yourself answer, you must make sure that you are not pretending, that you are not giving yourself what you want to hear, that you are not assuming God's will for you. Because you like the pretty woman and you say, "I hear the pretty woman will be mine," does not mean she will be yours. She has her own free will and her own obligation to her worth. You are never taught that you have dominion over others, or their free will. That will never be our teaching. What we do teach, though, is the witnessing and the perception of the one before you in her own divinity as the aspect of the Creator manifested in form, and your choice to see it illumines you and changes your world.

If you go to a store where there are a million people, or a hundred million people, all seeking for their bargains, looking for what is theirs, looking to how to get what they need, that is the world you see. If you can imagine, for a moment, standing in that store and realizing, and we underline *realizing*, that each and every person there is acting on the level of consciousness that they hold, and the ones hoarding food are operating in lack, and the ones pushing in line are operating in fear, and the ones afraid to take what they want because they don't feel worthy are operating in the significance that they have held as their self-esteem. So go there, in that store, and imagine, all of the sudden, that the radio that you are is changing stations, and the vibration that emanates as you begins to fill the whole place:

> "I know who you are, I know what you are, I know how you serve."

and instills in all the consciousness of the Christ. You will be amazed, we say, at what you perceive, and the ones before you, in fact, will be changed, but by their own authority. The aspect of them that recognizes the song you sing, the Christ within them, the divinity within them, has been so hungry for this song that they will begin to attend to it, and they will start to move into accord. The one hoarding will give away, the one pushing ahead will stop, the one frightened to claim will give herself what she needs, because that is the manifestation of the Christ that can be made so with you operating as the expression of it.

"Now the store," Paul is asking, "is that a metaphor for our plane?" In some ways, yes, but it is much more a metaphor of how you all attend to yourselves in consciousness. You are all in this thing together, like it or not. The music that plays in the background, we say, will inform the actions of the ones hearing the music. You become an orchestra, all of you who attend to our teaching, you become an orchestra playing in fullness. And each time one of you aligns to the Word, "I am Word through all that I see before me," you support others in waking up and joining the song.

The orchestra is playing already, you know. We are singing through Paul, we are singing through the world in what ways we can, and you are singing as well. You are already in immanence, and you are already in consciousness. Your vibration is already calling your reality to you, so the significant change, we say, is the intention. "I see all that I see before me in love," correlates to an expression of love in all that you see before you.

Now, this is not just something that the individual does to change her own perception. When you have been attuned to the vibration of the Word and, in fact, you have been, if you have attended to our teachings, what you are doing is expressing the Word in all that you see before you. You are expressing love as love, and the majesty that you bring forward is received by those ready to receive it.

We will say one thing, and it is very important: This is not a religion. We would never want that. This is an attendance to truth that may be known as and through you, and it is free to all. You don't need a penny to claim the Word as you. You simply need the intention, and the willingness to go where you are called to go, and to leave behind that leather bag, that bag of tricks that has gotten you though your life thus far, that was attended to in fear, collected out of necessity as a way to defend, as a way to achieve, as a way to feel yourself perceived by one way or another. You are not your stuff, and your physical stuff is stuff, your emotional stuff is stuff and the stuff that you think you need, the ways of getting by, you don't need those as well. What is falling away is only what is no longer required. Do you understand this?

If there is something that you require in your history that is of benefit, you would never let it go. There is a reason you learned it in the first place. If you speak French, that comes in very handy in France. You learn that at a time, it is your information, it is not your history. A history is a frame, it's a way of perceiving the world based on external requirements, or things that have happened to you that support you in holding a worldview that is not necessarily accurate.

The first step is to say, "It may be different than I see," and, in this way, you align to what may be so. Now who you are as you say you are will always transform your expression. Who you thought you were is what has given you what you have today. If it is serving you well, so be it. But we will tell you one thing: The revolution you are attending to within yourself dismantles even those things that you have relied upon to give you solace or a sense of control over the world around you. And the simple reason they are being dismantled is that they were born in fear, or they do not allow you to lift beyond the platform that you already attend to.

When you rise in frequency, what goes with you is what is in accord with that same level of vibration. If the vibration of the choice is high, you will carry it with you. If it is an old vibration that is no longer high, was created at a time when it was needed, it will be left behind. You will find yourself in a new plane, and a new plane, we say, is a new experience of yourself on this plane that you exist in in higher consciousness. You lift above the world that you have known to see the true world that has always been there. The kingdom, we say, is at hand, but it has always been here, unperceived but by few.

As many of you wake up to who you are, how you see your-selves and the ones beside you creates a great opening for the human beings you are to align to your next level of an evolutionary process. As you know yourselves primarily through physical form now, you have great reliance on the physical plane, and you create laws to protect the physical plane. The spiritual plane, we say, does not adhere to the laws of man; it adheres to the laws of spirit. And as you sing your song, you unshackle yourself from the evolution that was stopped when you were told you were not allowed to sing.

Now we will stop in a few moments, but we have one thing to say to Victoria, who has been very attentive through these sessions, and who is a wonderful student. Any fear that you have of the freedom that we speak of is a fear that you have of yourself. And this is true for each of you. "There will be chaos if all men are in choice." In fact, all men are already in choice in whatever way they can be, and choosing the choice to be free in consciousness liberates the entire being. You still have to pay your parking ticket if you speed, but you know you are choosing to do it, and if you do not do it, you are choosing that in your integrity.

The violence each man has held against his brother, in many

ways, is not a product of free will and the divine acting in man. It is the choice of fear to be demonstrated as fear. It is the action of fear, which, we say, seeks to replicate itself as and through you.

When you understand this, that the fear that you hold of the self, all of you, is the fear you see expressed outside of you, you begin to transform. The revolution is at hand, yes, and it is a good revolution, but it is the revolution of spirit, in knowing, in Christ consciousness. And the level of Christ consciousness we speak of holds no harm, holds no judgment, holds no ill will. It cannot be so. When enough of you are attending to this level of vibration, there is a planetary shift, a causal shift, and the world begins to sing.

Now Paul is already getting in the way, "Oh no, that was a world prophecy, it cannot be so." It will be so, and we will tell you why: The aspect of the Creator within you already knows that this may be so. And as we said to you earlier in the text, once something becomes a possibility, it may be claimed and materialized. The new world you see before you has been prophesized. It already exists, you know. We are simply taking you to a plane that lives with you concurrently that has been precluded from your perception by a lens of fear and external control. So it will be so, we say, because it is already so. The sick will be healed, the hungry will be fed, and you will know love.

We will attend to this teaching again when we resume. We will speak tomorrow if we can, if not, as soon as possible. Thank you each and good night. Stop now, please.

Day Sixteen

We teach as we can. As we are aligned to you, as you hear us, as we recognize you in your merit, you stand before yourselves and you awaken to a possibility: "I may know myself in a new way, I may see myself in a new way, and as I see myself in a new way, I see the world before me anew."

Congratulations to each of you. We will say this now. You have lived a life up until today that you have claimed, you have accepted, you have decided upon. And now you will move on. You will move on to a new way of expressing yourself as the one who may call to her love and freedom. Now you don't think this is a promise that may come true because you still have an inkling of doubt that this teaching may be meritful. And we will remind you of one thing: The inkling of doubt that you like to hold on to is enough to pull the curtain down and obscure yourself from the view that is now being opened to. So we will attend to the inkling of doubt right now:

"On this day I choose to allow myself to be in receipt of my own divine worth and claim my power as the one who may know himself, herself, in choice. And as I align to my own freedom of choice, I claim my worth and I activate myself in accord with my knowing of my inheritance. My inheritance, I say, is my knowing, my worth, my claim of freedom and my love. I know this is so, I accept this is so, and

I live my life in accordance with this claim. I am Word through this intention. Word, I am Word."

In this moment you are bringing your own vibration to repair any dis-ease you may have, any fabrications you may hold, any misgivings you may harbor that you cannot be so, that you cannot be recognized by yourself as the one in worth in his claim, her claim of knowing.

Now we say, "Congratulations," for all you have known, and we move it to the side. We move it to the side so that we may call forth the new creation that may be born as you and through all that you see. The lives that you know have been inherited by you in fear. What is a life that is not fear? What is a life that is not in creations born in fear? We will tell you what it is: It is the kingdom of God as may be perceived by you and through you and made anew.

Now what happens to the world you know at this alignment? We must explain this to you, as you are the perceiver and the one who calls to you creation, and you understand that what you decide before you you have claimed, you must understand that what is before you must be new in the new claim you make. The vision that you hold that has yesterday's newspaper plastered upon the windowpane will give you yesterday's news. So we take you up, we move the pane; we move the windshield, if you like, to be in accord with what is now before you.

The kingdom, we say, is a creation of consciousness that may be manifested upon this plane by each of you. The collective vision of many who hold this sight bring to bear on the conscious reality of this entire plane a new foundation upon which is built the Christ in manifestation in all things.

Now understand this, please: The teaching we are giving you is very important. To speak of the kingdom means the manifestation of God in all things as can be perceived by man, as is created by man, as will be known. And you say these words, "I know who I am, I know what I am, I know how I serve," in recognition of your aspect, as the Christ come to bear upon you and all you see. How you witness—and that is the name of this chapter, "How You Witness"—will call to you your perceptions made so.

The foundation of God is built already upon truth and what is not in truth will no longer be, and we will tell you how: When the rising of this vibration on this plane moves into accord with the evolution of man as we see it, the physical plane is moored in agreement with this, and the manifestations that may be held on this plane must go into agreement with that which is of God. And we say truth must be said, must be claimed, must be witnessed.

Now, how do you witness and perceive truth? Through an incarnation of yourself in truth. As you embody in the higher vibration, you see truth because you are in accord with truth. What is no longer in truth, what no longer adheres to this vibration, will be released because it cannot be sustained by your vibration. When a collective vibration, when many go into a vibration in agreement with truth, they create a vortex that spins and calls to them what needs to be transformed. The witnessing you do, that you each do, of your fellows, of yourself as you face yourself, and of those things that mankind has created in worth, claim you in value, in identity. As the truth you are is expressed, it is claimed, it is responded to, and the life you live is transformed.

Now collective identity, we say, is a new thing to talk about. The differentiations that you have each held by who you say you are, your racial identity, your ancestry, your religious identity, is all well and good, but you must understand that that is a small view of the self, and as the small view of the self operates as a frame, it by its nature excludes other things. When you have a painting in a frame, it holds a vision of something. The pretty sky may be seen in a painting, but if the painting were twenty feet longer you would see so much more. Frames are used to discriminate reality.

When you have a religion that says such and such is so, you frame a reality. When you have an identity that says, "My family has always done and believed," you frame a reality. Now, we do not ask you to abandon those aspects of the self that have been framed, we ask you to see beyond the frame, those aspects of you may be included—the sexual identity you hold, the color of your hair, the things that you believe make you you—they are not lost, they are included in the magnificence of all that can be seen.

When you decide on a creation that you will adhere to, "My name is such and such, I live at such and such a place, and these are the things I claim as myself," you may be very self-satisfied in the world that you choose, but you may be doing this at the cost of a great vision, a great witnessing of how much more there is. To learn to discern what is habituated, "I have always believed such and such because that was our truth, our people's truth, our culture's truth," will give you permission to go beyond that structure.

Now, the structure you see before you every day is acclimating to you as a result of conscious projection and, yes, unconscious projection as well—those things that you hold secret within yourself that still find their way to be out-pictured. For example, yes, the secret belief that you are not worthy, the belief that you cannot have this or that, these are the things that you claim. The identity that you know yourself through is so much greater than you have given yourself permission to know. As you idealize the truth "I know who I am, what I am, how I serve," your creations move into agreement with this on both a conscious and subconscious level. The whole identity, we say, is accepted by the vessel of the Christ.

Now the Christ, we say, *as* you, is the key. And we will say this again: *the Christ as you.* You do not become the Christ, the Christ becomes you. And Christ, as we say it, is a state of conscious manifestation of the truth of who you are, in immanence in conscious choice and in witnessing of all that you see and know. "I know who I am" is this claim, "what I am" is this claim, "how I serve" is the expression of this claim.

Now we will answer a couple of questions about what has

come so far. "What does it mean to be the Christ?" says the woman who is frightened of the terminology, or believes that everyone will be running around the house saying, "No, I'm the Christ!" "No, she's the Christ!" "Who's the Christ?" Well, guess what? You are all the Christ. The true identity of mankind in his Son-ship is the Christ and the song has begun to be heard.

The awakening is happening individually and collectively on this continent and the next and the one beside it. As you know what you are, you perceive this in others, and the collective choice becomes to witness in love, so see in worth, and in the knowing of who and what you are.

What will happen to the world when enough of you collectively know what you are? We will tell you. You will know yourselves as you truly are, as you have always been. We know who you are because we are you, in many ways. We are who you evolve into as you become aware of yourselves in truth. We know you because we know who we are.

Now, what happens on this plane? How does it transform? Those of you who recognize who you are, who hold a level of vibration that we will say is in accord with the Christ will live a life of worth and truth and knowing. Those of you who deny this will find a way to replicate what they have known and that will be their truth. There is no division, really. As we have said in other texts, all men eventually come home to the heart of the Creator, and your free will, as we said, is sacred and will always be honored. But how one of you perceives an experience based in her level of consciousness and, consequently, responds to it may be quite different from one who disassociates herself from her own worth and therefore the worth of those she sees before you.

We will not speak of cataclysm as a future for this culture or this plane because we do not recommend it as a creation to give attention to. We will tell you this, though: The identity of man as one in knowing will claim vibration that will alter the course of history as has been projected by those who would stay in fear. And those who wish to stay in fear will do what they can to continue to perpetuate fear as a way of living.

When you understand that when you lift above fear, you lift above the manifestations of fear and fear can no longer consume you, you create at a higher level of consciousness. Now we will tell you this: Lower vibration will lift when there is justification, when enough of you have claimed to merit it as the new known, as what may be accepted and perceived. We will ask you if you want it, and if you do, we will say, "Yes, it can be."

As we have said before, what we are teaching you is in accordance with truth. The high level of vibration that we instruct in is already manifest. You must go to that place of consciousness to be it. And in the being of it, you see it in all things.

Now the next question we would like to attend to is one of love and regret. "I have loved before and I have been harmed. My fear has proven me right so many times. I do not want to step in the sun because I know myself as safe in shadow. I hide my face in shadow so that I may not be seen as who I am. And although I understand the teaching being given to me, I will not live a life that must force me to be known in my worth by another." The fear of being known by God and the fear of being loved are presumptuous. We will tell you why:

To declaim the self as unworthy of love, to hide in the shadow while the light is before you is to presume that you know more than your Creator. And while the shadow may be there, the sun shines behind the shadow. What has obscured the light may be moved and will be attended to by us if you would allow us to help you. And by help, we mean attend to you where you are today. Today is important, because the knowing that you can hold will only be made so in the moment you stand in. So we would like to attend to you now, and we would like to attend to those of you who do not believe you can be loved and, consequently, do not believe that you can have the life that we speak to.

As we stand before each of you, we will create an emanation. We stand before the reader as a collective truth. And we bring ourselves in accord with God's will for you, a radiance that we say will express as you, to you, and through you by us as you say "Yes." What we are doing right now is holding you in love, and as we hold you in love, we give permission to the aspect of the self that would hide in shadow, to show her face, to show his face. And as the eyes rise, they see the hand extended before them. And we take your hand in ours, and we bring you to the heart of God, to the love of Creator, that may be known through us as you, as each of you.

As we hold you in love, we say "Yes." Yes, it is so. Yes, it is so. Yes, it is so. And we offer ourselves to you as ones who may cherish you so that you know you may be cherished. As you know you will be cherished by us, you may allow yourself to be lifted and seen. And as you are witnessed in love by all that is, you are received by it, and we say "Yes" to you as well. You are who you say you are in your magnificence, in your beauty, in your claim of truth.

Now we will ask you this: Who doesn't know who they are? Who has attended to our words thus far who does not know who she is? If this question remains in your heart, open your heart to the answer. Allow it to be filled. We sing your song for you now as you are witnessed. We sing your song for you now as you are chosen. We sing your song for you now as you are loved.

We ask you this: Will you stand with us? Will you stand beside us now as you move into your own mastery, your own claim of identity, so that we may heal the world together? We thank you for your presence today. We will speak with you soon. Good night. Stop now, please.

Day Seventeen

We respect you each as you choose, and we modify our teachings as we assess your progress, as we assess your ability to relocate your consciousness in a higher way. Many of you struggle still because you cannot imagine releasing aspects of the self that you have held dear. Paul is interrupting already, "Don't we need to accept those aspects of the self?" Yes, you do. We are not abnegating anything, nor are we dislocating aspects of you. But we are telling you this: Your modifications to your own energy field are made in accordance with what you will allow. When you do not allow something to change, you do not change. We do not override your free will, but we escort you forward and we lift you as you are allowed so you may adhere to the new vision that is presented before you. And in that presentation you must witness what truly is.

The aspects of you that you are so overly attached to were born in need, at times of fear, at times when you needed to survive, or change, and didn't know the way through it. We will tell you now that those behaviors, while they may have served you at one time, are now standing in the way of your ability to choose what you might without them.

How do you decide to be free of fear when you believed fear was your only protection? How do you invite someone in to share your life when you believe you will be harmed if you do? How do you choose anew how to be in the world when all the information you have ever been given, whether or not it's served you well, is what is standing before you and, in some ways, obscuring the view of what may be possible?

Now when we said we modify our teaching, we do not mean that we lower our standards. We do mean that we find another way to lift you up and above the walls you have erected that would keep you from liberty, keep you from freedom, keep you from choosing something new. And the decision we have made, to attend to each of you as you stand before yourselves today, is to decide with you that anything is possible. And we want to underline this: *Anything is possible.* The moment you can believe this concept, you create a chasm in the wall that you have built around those things that would preclude you from freedom, that would stop you from embracing the new possibility, and that would shield you from love.

So we say this: Anything is possible. To decide right now that this is your new claim for the day will attend to the possibility that anything is possible and, consequently, can be known by you. And we say this with some strength: When you know that anything is possible, you claim your own identity in accordance with this:

"I am the one who knows that anything may be possible, can be claimed, can be chosen."

The attendance that you have to those things you have known, that you have become overly attached to, or are frightened of dismantling, will be known by you as you work with yourself in reflection.

What you perceive around you, in many ways, is an accurate reflection of your consciousness. The pictures on the wall, the flooring beneath you, you have all accepted, you exist in, you respond to as your own. Those things beyond the structure you live in, the roads, the highways, the billboards on the high-ways, the people that you encounter on your road, are also in acceptance of your freedom as the one who chooses to be in the encounter. So if you understand, first and foremost, that everything that you see you are in accord with, in one way or another, you can begin to see those aspects of you that are standing in the way of your liberation as a consciousness.

Now your life, we say, and how you know your life, is a state of awareness of your consciousness that you have chosen to be in regard with. Your entire life, we say, has been chosen by you to know yourself through. So to align yourself to the new ideal, "Anything is possible," re-creates those things that were once held in form, in material form, as standing firm, to be realigned to a new way of being.

The reason we attend to this teaching today is that we are intending to call you each forward with your own missions, your own alignment, to decide that you can heal yourselves and, consequently, heal the world before you. The attendance to these needs, those things that stop you from the path you choose, are now mandatory for the one who wants to decide that she is aligned to her path.

Many days we hear people, and they come and they say, "Who are we?" and we say, "Who do you think you are?" They say, "What am I here for, what is my work?" And we say, "What do you want to spend your time doing?" You must know, each of you, that what you align to is what you have agreed with, what you believe you can hold, and what you claim as you and your own. Unless you re-create the self in higher regard, you do not re-create the life you live. One goes in hand with the other.

Now what is your true purpose? Why did you come into this incarnation? As we have said many times, your true purpose, each man's true purpose, each being's true purpose, is to align to their higher nature—if you wish, the Christ within—and demonstrate it as who you are in encounters, in witnessing, in all ways. This assignment is not just for you or for the readers of our text. It is for all humans to know who they are and witness their fellows in the same way. What you do with your time, how you choose to make your living, what you claim for yourself is your choice. But going back to a message we have given before, we must always encourage you to ask yourself why you choose what you choose, and when you are in attendance to what you have been taught, question the validity of the teaching.

When someone wants to know who they are in higher consciousness, the first person to ask is the self, because the self holds the answers, and not necessarily the answers you will want to know. The self knows the fears, because the self has created the fears and reinvested in them until they have become structures that have stood in the way of the progress you say you seek.

Now as we witness you, as we stand before you and call you forward, we undermine those structures by our very presence. The acclimation we hold to higher consciousness is not in accord with the creations of man that were born in lower frequency. Consequently, we do not exist in the same plane as creations born in fear. While we understand that you do, we are able to extend a hand and to lift you in consciousness and in vibration to this plane of knowing—if you wish, the Christ consciousness or the awareness of the divine in all things—so that you, too, will know the new world that may be benefited from your presence.

The new world, we say, or, if you wish, the kingdom, is not only at hand, it is always present, but may only be perceived by one in accord with his own divine nature. Now, the retributions that you hold against yourselves, the denial of worth, the shame that you hide behind, the crucifixions that you entitle yourself to as a way of knowing yourself, in fact, are not needed. They are not requirements for attending to yourself at this new level of awareness. In fact, they cannot attend to you at this level of consciousness because they don't exist there.

Now Paul is interrupting, "Are you saying that when we ascend to a higher level of vibration, we will not experience fear, or shame, or regret?" You have the right to, if you like, but those things are not in accord with the level of vibration we are teaching and, consequently, you will have to go back down to align to them. They are creations, in many ways, and, in fact, formulas of processing experience that you have abided by. Who says you have to be ashamed for something that you have done? Who says you have to live a life of regret? Who says you are not entitled to joy? When you answer those questions to yourself, you may attend to the answers as your experience.

Now when we align to the high vibration and we witness those things before us, we see you in what you have created, what you imagine yourselves to be and, consequently, what you out-picture and claim as your own. When we witness you, we do not align to those things that you hold in obstacle, that you attach to, out of habit, or in fear. We see you in your worth, your perfection, and your true alignment: the divine perfection that was first created as you.

We are witnessing the entirety of you. We don't dismantle those things that you need to accept, or you need to decide whether or not you still need, we see the entirety of you, but we align to your divinity, because that is the aspect of the self that will be lifted. And in this lifting, those other things that have been attended to in fear and shame no longer exist.

Now the castle that you stand in has a moat around it, and it is a moat of separation. The castle has a door, and you may walk out and walk on the countryside and have your encounters, but most of you still exist behind the castle wall. And you stand in the turrets with your binoculars and look for the next bad thing that can happen to you. That is a habit. And as you look for trouble, you call trouble to you. And if you don't see trouble, you will find a reason to make it.

The turret is not a real structure. You are lifted high enough to see the valley, but you are still looking for those things that exist in lower frequency. When we rise with you, we rise above the trouble to an element of fear that no longer exists and has been transmuted by your presence to be seen for what it truly was, simply love. In the face of love, in the face of divine presence, all creations are known in a new way. The thing that would have frightened you so much when you were in lower vibration is no longer in accord with you and, consequently, cannot be attended to by you in this new vibration.

We will say that the world that you exist in has been created by each of you, individually and collectively, according to the laws that have governed you, and the religions that you have abided by, and the history that you share. But the plan for you and the plan for this plane, we say, is one of light and re-creation. And as you attend to yourselves as we teach you, we create anew the passage that you will walk through to be attended to in your worth, in your knowing, and in your freedom.

Now what are the requirements for the teaching today? What do we need to gift you with so that you may know what to do? As we said, the first assignment is "anything is possible," and by doing this you expand the possibilities. And you also unconsciously untie yourselves from the structures that you have attended to, built and created and agreed with, that you believe to be permanent.

There is one problem that you have, each of you, that you believe cannot be surmounted. Now, when you move this to possibility, in fact, what you have moved is the exchange of consciousness between you and your creation. You are giving it permission to realign. To redecide on your own that this may be so will shift the object of your attention. There is no other way.

Now we will ask you each to do one thing today, which is to recognize that you have chosen these things, these things that you hold that you have tied yourselves to. You have accepted them for real as what you have made in order to protect yourself, or to know yourself through. The moment you take responsibility for this, you are no longer a victim to those things but a participant, and the one that can change her mind in the face of expression, in the face of new possibilities, in the face of choice.

Now to your detriment, most of you respond by saying, "It's too much for me. Where do I start?" As we said, choose one thing to re-create in the new claim we have gifted you with, "Anything is possible," and align to that and see what you feel. If you immediately dismiss it, and walk away and re-embrace your issue, hold it tightly to yourself in arrogance in the face of a new choice, you will see very quickly how attached you are to what you have chosen. The moment you realize that you are the one holding these things is the moment that you can give yourself permission to release them.

Habits form in many ways and they become unconscious behavior. So much of what you do is habit that you do not question the benefits of the thing you engage with. As we teach you, we walk you forward. The hand is reaching to you, and today anything is possible.

As we attend to you now, we will question your regard and your attachment to what you have known. When there is an incident in your life that has caused you pain, and you hold it in memory in service to protect you from future pain, you have aligned to pain. Now, we are not saying that experience should not be your teacher, and in fact, experience is your teacher. But when we say you are not your history, we are telling you that the abnegation of self to pain, the abnegation of choice to what you have known, the deferment of the new choice in light of the old is what we are asking you to choose anew. When you create from your history, you re-create what you have known. But you align to these things in your history because you believe you must.

Now when we walk you forward and we offer you the mission we would like to give you, we can only claim you in your own authority. We can beckon you forward but we cannot make you walk.

"On this day I decide to realign my frequency to this new knowledge that anything is possible. On this day I witness all things before me as in transformation, as in healing, as in a new way of being engaged with my expression. As I choose to know all things as possible, I reclaim my power and my ability to perceive those structures I have known as permanent in a new way, and I align to my freedom as the one who chooses her life, his life, anew. I am Word through this intention. Word I am Word."

As we leave you today, we would like to leave you with a new thought. The regard you hold for your fellows as unable to change is a direct reflection of what you believe about your-selves. "They will never change" is an act of arrogance. You do not know. "I will never change" is a claim of truth. And if you say that they will never change, you are deciding for them that who they are is impenetrable by Source. If anything is possible, they are possible too, and the transformation of all, all mankind, may be accepted as a true possibility.

We leave you now. We will speak with you soon. Thank you and good night. Stop now, please. Period.

NINE

THE DOORWAY[5]

Day Eighteen

Ask yourself questions tonight and see what you know. See how you abnegate your own authority as the one who cannot know. You don't even ask yourself the right questions anymore. You assume you will not know the answer if you ask yourself what you are here for, how you can find love, how you can choose a life. You forget to ask because you diminish your own power as the one who may not know herself as the one who may claim the kingdom.

Now we speak of the kingdom in our text, we speak of the kingdom to our students and the kingdom, we say, is the recognition of your own divinity and the divinity in all. That is the kingdom, and it is at hand, and it is present now. It always has been. You have not lifted your eyes to be able to perceive. The

---

5 This chapter was delivered while Paul was conducting his regular Thursday night group.

questions you must ask yourself now are, "Am I allowed?" "Do I believe myself worthy of?" "Will I take myself where I am invited to go?"

We are opening a doorway for you now. It is a big doorway. You may all fit through. You don't have to frighten yourselves that you will not make it to the call. You must align only to the decision that you have that you are free to acclimate to what is beyond the doorframe. What is beyond the doorframe, we say, is you in higher vibration. What stands between you and the doorframe are all those things you have decided are greater than you that will not be changed that keep you imprisoned to your history, or to your fear, or the belief that you cannot be who you say you are. There is nothing else there that is stopping you anymore from claiming your future as the one who is aligned at this level of provenance.

Now we ask you this: What do you think you are? What does your mind tell you when you inquire? What is the answer you receive from yourself, and what do you need to know about your lives to be able to make up your own minds and call yourself forward to be in your freedom in the way that we express? There is no one in this room, there is no one on this plane, who is unworthy of this.

As some of you know this and go into accord with it, you expand the doorframe so that more may enter. Do you understand this? You are a way-shower, yes, but you cannot show the way if you don't go, if you don't go where you are called. And we are speaking to him as much as you, who holds the telephone and worries, "Can it be so?" [6] It has always been so, it will always be so, the only difference from these times is that the invitation is asking you, is beckoning you forward.

Now, what does it mean to say "No"? It means to play small. It means to pretend that you are not worthy. And we say "pretend" intentionally, because if you knew your worth, your inherent worth, you would know that anything else is a lie. It has to be a lie if, in fact, you are who you say you are, an aspect of the Creator in her manifestation, in her realization of her immanence.

Now we ask you this: Who do you want to be? What does your mind tell you? "I want to be a famous musician." "I want to be a happy wife." "I want to be the one all the boys are after." It doesn't really matter. But when you look at your victories, and those things that you would claim, you will see how small they are and how rooted in history they have always been. Why do you want all the boys? Why do you want to be the happy wife? Why must others know your worth as a musician for you to validate your own?

Now, we are not speaking to you individually. You are all very creative people. You all have lives. We do not diminish your dreams. But when we say, "What do you want?" and you say, "I want my spaghetti dinner," as if that is the result of your prayer, you do not get much more, because we can only gift you and take you where you allow yourselves to go. So there is

---

6 The Guides are addressing Paul here.

nothing wrong with wanting things, but there is much wrong with diminishing the self, as we explain.

Paul is interrupting right now. He says, "Is this a chapter for the text?" and we say, it may well be. We have much to teach, you have much to learn, we have much to share with our students about what they say they want.

Now the crises you all engage with, "I cannot be loved," "I want the wrong things," "I am not as spiritual as I should be. If I was, I would want what they say I should want," is a mistaken way of understanding what we are saying. You can choose whatever you like. Your life is your own choice. But only ask yourself this: If you are being invited to a great party, a great celebration of your true soul, why would you stay at home and wonder if you were allowed? We are inviting you now. We are calling you forward. We are deciding you may be as you choose, as you decide, as you stand in your freedom as the one who may walk through the doorway.

Now, what is the doorway? The doorway is the passage between what you have known and what you may accept as you in higher vibration. It is a symbolic choice, to walk through a doorway, but it is an actual expression that has physical ramifications. When you walk from one room to the next, you see a different view. There may be a different window on the wall, there may be a different teaching waiting for you. But if you don't enter the new room, you will not attend to those things. They will not be available to you. You will say, "I am not allowed."

Now the fear that you each have of stepping through the doorway, of claiming your power as the one who may do this, is that there is nothing on the other side of the door. What would that mean? "I go through all this trouble. I pray, and I fast. I worry and I claim. I make decisions in accord with what I have been taught. And here, I walk through a doorway, and there is no other room. The room is the same as I just left."

Why would we disappoint you? What benefit would that be? If you are still seeing the room you left, you have never left the room. Do you understand this? You may say you're on a diet, but if you still feed yourselves the cake, that is your diet, and you reap the results of that diet. Do you understand this?

So when you stand on the threshold of a new choice and you claim your power as the one who may do this, you align to great possibility, and achievement, we say, is the result of the possibility you have invited. Achievement in many ways: achievement in manifestation, achievement in love, achievement in worth, and all of these things are simply saying, "You have inherited the kingdom." The kingdom is here. It has always been here. It lies right beyond this doorway.

Now what you ask for you are in agreement with. "I want my mother to love me," because you believe you need her love. "I want my body to be beautiful all the time, until I am a hundred years old," may be your claim and desire because you are in accord with your wishes. But you dance around the rooms that you have existed in, and you find the mirror that reflects what you want, and that is what you stand before. "This is how

I have known myself. This is how I believe myself to be." You look for your mirror to affirm who you have been, not who you are, and who you have claimed to be, "I know who I am."

Now we ask you this: If you were to stand in a doorway to a new vibration, a new way of being expressed as you, what would hinder you from stepping forward? As we said, the fear that there will be no new room certainly is one, but that is not the real one, and that is not the real fear. The real thing that keeps you back is the belief that you are not worthy of the kingdom.

Now we will do something for you, and we will do something for everybody who hears these words. We will tell you something different and we will claim you in a new way. We know who you are, we know why you have come, we know how you serve. We know how you stand in your merit, how you decide, how you lay claim to your future, and how you love. We know who you are and, if you give us the right, right now, we will do this for you. We will say these words and we will announce them to the world:

To all who hear our voice, to all who say "Yes," to all who claim the kingdom, we ring a bell. And the bell is an annunciation of all that will be, and a renunciation of all that has been. And in the vibration of the bell that we bring into being, we clear the frequency of each one who hears our voice of the manifestation of fear of being in her own worth, of fearing herself, as believing, herself, himself, to be unworthy of love and the creation of the kingdom that is now at hand.

. . .

Now the words we speak are being spoken to your hearts. The words we speak are being spoken to your souls. The words we speak are being spoken to you throughout time so that you may dismantle the structures that you hold that keep you in your purview as the one who is not allowed to step over the threshold.

Imagine now that we stand before you each, and as we claim your purview, as we see you in your worth, as you choose to go with us, you stand, you rise, and you raise your voice to say, "Yes."

> "Yes, I am. Yes, I am worthy. Yes, I hear my own words and I declaim that I am no longer willing to set foot in my history as my present. I decide that I am no longer willing to limit my expression by what I was told I once was, that I will live my life in accordance with my frequency that I lay claim to on the other side of the threshold."

The manifestation of God as man is the kingdom made manifest. Do you hear our words? The manifestation of God in man is the kingdom made manifest. And how you attend to these words in consort with your own soul's worth is what gives you the right to incarnate at the level we speak of. Now damn yourselves all you want to. Unforgive yourselves all you believe you must. That does not change a thing. You are still worthy, you are still worthy, you are still loved.

So we will ask you this: We will ask the listener this, the reader, if you like. As you stand before the door, imagine the doorframe is filling with light, is filling with light and the light calls you forward. As you stand in the doorway you claim victory. You hear the bell ring and you move your own vibration into accord with its peal. You sing the song of the bell, "I know who I am, I know what I am, I know how I serve," and you step forward to claim manifestation.

Now you will feel this. You will feel your vibration transform as the one who said "Yes." And as you feel this, let it align you at a molecular level to who and what you have always been: a perfect child of the Creator who knows her name, who knows his name.

"I sing my song in worth. I see my destiny before me. I see the kingdom as it is made manifest in my expression, and I witness the world before me in transformation. I call myself to my new name: I know who I am, I know what I am, I know how I serve. And I sing the song to my fellows, as I perceive their face. I know who you are, we are of the same frequency. I know what you are, we are of the same flesh. I know how you serve as you express yourself, in your beauty, in your choice to be seen. As I am your witness, I know who you are as Word. I am Word through the ones I see before me. Word, I am Word."

Now we will teach you something, now. You have changed your mind. You have stepped ahead. If you look behind you,

you will see the light that you walked into. You will not see what was. You will witness the light that you stepped forward in.

If you elect to go back over the doorframe, at least you know your way now. It doesn't go away. But as you witness what you were, you see her, you see him, you see all that you have known in the eyes of the Christ. And the eyes of the Christ, we say, holds no judgment, holds no fear, hold no malice, because it is not in accord with the vibration it knows. Do you understand this, yes? As we say "Yes" to you, you say "Yes" to all that will be.

We have given you each a mission, to be in the light, to regard your fellows in worth, and as you have stepped over the doorframe beyond the threshold of what was, you are entitled to some new directions. So in the subsequent chapters we dictate, we will begin to offer you the directions for the lives that you may live. Until now, you have spoken your name as framed by your birth. Until now, you have seen your face as framed by your heritage, by that which you have known. Now we say, "Yes," we make all things new. And in this new way, you perceive yourselves, and your lives, and your beauty as they truly are. You are loved, you are seen, and you are cared for.

Now ask what you want. If you still want the plate of spaghetti, you still may well get it. But if you want the kingdom, it is here. It is here. It is here. We thank you each for your presence. We will stop this part of the teaching now. We will come back with you in your own way, as you have been attended to in the past. Thank you for your presence and good night. Stop now, please.

(Pause)

Now we will take their questions. What do they need to know about their work, about what we have taught, about what you have claimed? You may ask this, please.

Q: *We are the kingdom because we are the expression of an aspect of the Creator?*

The kingdom is the manifestation of God in man as perceived by you in all things. It is another level of consciousness that may be attended to as you have claimed it. It is not a place you go to on a map, it is another expression of consciousness that may be attended to by you as you know who you are. Do you understand this, yes?

Q: *What about the keys to the kingdom?*

You are the key to the kingdom! Why do you have to make it hard? We gave you an open doorway—we walked you through. Now he wants the key! The door was opened for you. What do you think we are doing here? If you want the key, go back and find one! Perhaps you may close the door as you go and try to get the right key in the lock. There is no need, there is no need, there is no need.

What is the next question, please?

Q: *As we choose the kingdom, we have the kingdom as we see it, or we have our history and our habits, and the kingdom is something that we access through our claiming, through our knowing?*

You left your history, you transformed yourself and here you want to bring it back with you! Well, you just said so: "We *have* our history," means you still hold it. You don't have to hold it anymore.

What you are doing when you cross the threshold is reclaiming yourself in the face of what you have known in order to leave it behind you. As we said, those ways of self-identifying that stop you from your work, your claim of manifestation, is what we have had to attend to, to deliver you from what you have claimed in the past.

Now don't understand yourself to be wrong through your question. What we do say to you is: The embodiment and incarnation of the self in frequency at a level of awareness that you may demonstrate is the key to the kingdom, is the manifestation as you. If you wish to damn your fellows, you might as well go back home to that level of awareness where damnation exists. Why would you think that damnation would exist in the level of vibration we attend to? It does not. If you wish to return there, you have to go back to that level of mind where such things may be.

You may ask another question.

Q: *Where we are right now, in this frequency that I'm experiencing right now, it's just a matter of being in . . . ? I don't have experiences yet in this . . .*

We said we would teach you how to work with the frequency and how to step forward in the new vibration, so you must be patient. We set you out into the new room, and she wants to tour the entire house already. That may come in time. Why don't you get used to where you stand now?

Somebody else, please. Who wants to know something about the work tonight?

Q: *I keep hearing, "Resurrection, the resurrection of Christ." I don't know if it's Easter or something else, but it feels like it's the awakening of Christ inside of us.*

In all men. The Christ, as we have said, and will say again, is the aspect of God that may be realized as and through

you. That is who you each are, in your remarkable selves. So
yes, we attend to the awakening and, if you like, the resurrection. We have an issue already with the readers of our
work who throw the book aside because of the language we
use, and what they perceive to be Christian dogma that we
are attending with in our teachings. In fact, that is not what
we are saying.

You must understand that there are great myths on this
plane that are born in great truth. And if you try to believe
them in literal ways, you will often miss the point. The
Christ is resurrected in all mankind as one knows who she
is and knows who her fellows are. That is the gift of the Creator and, if you like, the Christ.

Now ask yourself this: Who is not worthy of this? Who is
not worthy of this? Who is not worthy of this? If you have
the answer to that, you know you still have work to do. Do
you understand this? If you still would like to punish your
fellows, if you would still like to hold the keys to the jail
before them, you are not free yourselves. Attend to yourselves, we say, attend to your own knowing, so that you may
know your fellows as they truly are.

Is there a question, please?

Q: *I feel like I've experienced, had moments of experiencing the
kingdom, but I can't hold myself there for, I guess, longer periods
of time.*

You have to trust enough the level of vibration that you attend to. When you see a bird jump out of a nest, it doesn't fare very well until it learns that it can sustain itself in flight. On this plane, none of you were told that you could fly. We are teaching you, in a way, to work in elevated consciousness and you have created a civilization that would pull you down from the heights you stand at, at every opportunity. As you attend to yourself as the one in choice and you realign your vibration to what you truly are, you begin to exist at that level of freedom more than you know. And as it becomes more than you know, it becomes its new habit to sustain your frequency.

Now, as we have said many times, you are all radios. You spin your dial to and fro based on the response you have to external stimuli and emotional responses. As you are the victims of those things through your attachments to them or your judgment of them or your fear or rage or fury, you are in a predicament. Can you imagine a radio going back and forth and back and forth between the channels high and low? That becomes your broadcast. You must decide that you are the one who may attend to your vibration.

This does not mean you have to play the same channel all day long. Some of you need to get good and angry to realize you are worthy of what you want. Some of you need to weep so you may grieve what you once loved and move to the new love that may be waiting for you. It is not about being one thing. It is about being in your expression in your fullness, and in the requirement of that, of one who knows he's in choice. Do you understand this yes?

Is there another question, please?

Q: *If we don't know what we know, how can we know we are in the right place?*

If you don't know what you know, how can you know you are in the right place? Why don't you confuse yourself some more? What a lovely thing to do! Now, if you don't know something, you may move into your alignment:

"I am in my knowing. I am claiming myself in accordance with the answer I seek. I am being led to the right knowing that I require to know what I need, to claim my merit and choose wisely."

You may move into accordance with anything. As you are a radio, you choose your vibration. If you decide to go into accordance with fear, you vibrate in fear. If you decide to go into accordance with knowing, you vibrate in knowing and your knowing may be claimed by you. This does not mean you will have the solution to a problem the moment you may ask, it simply means you are receptive.

Now, there are things you don't need to know. As we have said before, some of you don't need to know how to cook. Somebody may cook for you. Somebody else may not know how to drive. You don't need a car. Somebody else may not need to know the circumstances that led to downfall of the empire of Rome, but you may look it up. You may find out how to bake a cake, or get behind the wheel of a car and learn. There is nothing that is not possible, if you decide you can align to it. Do you understand this, yes?

Is there another question, please?

Q: *How do you know when you are not standing in your worth?*

When you feel fear, when you are abnegating your power, and when you are looking for somebody else to tell you who you are because you don't trust what you know. Now, you may ask for help. We are not saying don't ask for help. But then claim yourself as worthy of the help you seek, do you understand this?

Is there another question, please?

Q: *It seems like there's a balance, maybe, that you would want. If you are in this room and you're embodied, you can also be experiencing a lot of other planes at the same time.*

What is your question, please?

Q: *Is there a technique to stay embodied here, or is that beneficial?*

The technique to stay embodied is to be yourself in high vibration. We have given you a system in embodiment:

"I am Word through my body, Word I am Word;
I am Word through my vibration, Word I am Word;
I am Word through my knowing of myself as Word,"

brings the higher frequency into accord with your manifested being. The claim of incarnation, "I know who I am, what I am, how I serve" supports you in expressing this as yourselves in all ways. There is not much more needed except knowing and worth, which is why that is the title of the book we are writing now, *The Book of Knowing and Worth.* Those are the keys to the answers you seek.

Is there another question, please?

Q: *Okay, what they're saying is all we need to know is what they're giving us. So what my question is, do we need to know about other things?*

If you want to learn Latin, go learn Latin, there is nothing wrong with learning Latin. Do you understand? There is not one way, or one system of information that is available to you. But what we are teaching you is embodiment, and expression as your Divine Self. That does not preclude other methods of learning. We would not be so selfish as to mandate that. If you want to learn Latin, there are many people to teach you. There are many languages, but they are all in expression of the same feelings. Do you understand this, yes? So the answer to that is, we are all one, and we do not discern what you may choose to be in your own process with.

Is there another question, yes?

Q: *I'm trying to learn about consciousness, and what I notice about myself is there are some things that I manifest easily, and then there's other things I can't seem to manifest at all. And when I sit with myself and try to understand what I'm doing differently, I don't get it. Can you help me? Is there something you can teach me about . . . ?*

We will teach the group because this was the teaching of the class. We are not doing individual work now. But you have a real question, which is what do you do when there are areas in your life where you are not manifesting? There are two reasons this happens: You don't believe you are worthy of it and don't want it, or it is not good for you to hold this in higher frequency at this time.

You may pray that you get the man of your dreams, and you may know who he is, you may know where he lives, and what he looks like. And should you get him, he would make your life a living hell. As you have been told, answered prayers are risky business.

Now, you may claim what you like and, as we have said many times, you must know why you want what you want in order to bring it into manifestation. We will say yes, sometimes it is just not time to have what you have claimed, and other times you don't really believe you want it or can hold it as your own vibration. If you can hold it as your own vibration, it is yours. If it is for your highest good, why wouldn't it be?

Is there a last question, please?

Q: *How do you know if you're just not self-worthy of that thing you're trying to manifest, or if it's just not time for you to hold it?*

Very good question. Ask, is the first thing. And understand that when you ask, the response that you get may not be what you like to hear. But yes, you must ask. Now, if you want something very badly and you are reaching for it and you don't believe you can have it, you have already created the possibility that you cannot have it, because you cannot hold it and be in accord with it. There is truth, we say, to those things that come to you readily because the way has been prepared for you.

One of the teachings we have given is that as you move into this level of alignment, what you call to you must be in accord with that level of vibration. You will get what you need because you know who you are. If you are demanding to feed off your brother's plate, you do not believe you will be provided for yourself. If you are jealous of what the one has beside you, you have already assumed that it is not for you and there must not be enough. If you disdain what your neighbors claim, because you believe you cannot have that yourself, you are playing games.

We have nothing against money, and we must say this: It is a symbol of exchange, and nothing more. We have nothing against beauty, but we see you all as beautiful. You see yourselves in ridiculous ways. How you measure your beauty based on popular ideals is quite fascinating to us. If you knew what you looked like to us, you would be very, very happy with yourselves, we promise you that.

Now we would like to thank you each. We will say we may include these questions in our text. They were very good questions and, with your permission, we may attend to them in a new way as we continue our work. We thank you each for your presence. We would like you to stand as one.

"I am Word through my body, Word I am Word.

I am Word through my vibration, Word I am Word.

I am Word through my knowing of myself as Word.

I am Word through all that I see before me."

Thank you each and good night.

III

═══════

TEN

THE KINGDOM

Day Nineteen

We will teach you now about our responsibility to the ordering of this text so that Paul may feel free to stop worrying about what goes in and what does not go in. It all goes in. We spoke last night to our students here and afar, and we will continue the teaching today on our chapter under the knowing that we are claiming the passage before you, and choosing to take you where we need you to go to be in your frequency, in your entitlement of what we have claimed for you.

Now we ask you, Paul, to step aside. We will give you the information we need now, and then we will begin the chapter that we would like to dictate. The chapter last night is "The Doorway," and that is the claim and the title of it. We begin a new chapter today about responsibility, and requirements of the individual to be in her authority regardless of what she encounters. You have all decided to take the step forward through the doorway. You have all said "Yes," you have all come forward.

Now understand, please, that by doing this you have decided to be the one who makes herself known being the responsible one to the challenges she may see before her. We ask you only one thing: to be yourselves as the one in charge. Do not be who you were taught you were, what you think you should be. You must decide that you are who you say you are and that that is what calls your future to you.

Now we will only say one thing to Paul, who is very worried today about his reception. The reception is perfectly fine. We do our job very well, despite how you feel. And the concerns you are feeling now are about the frames you would hold for how a book should be. We are the binding, and the authorship, and the producer of our texts, and if we do not like something, we will make it known.

Now, to be in responsibility simply means that you know that you are the one in charge of your own responses. You are the one who makes known what the requirements are for your being through every interaction you have. You are the one who believes that what is out-pictured before you is a creation that may be attended in accord with the new knowing that you hold. Now ask yourself this: Is there an aspect of my life that I put aside, that I disagree I am in control over? If that is the case, put this thing before you and look at your relationship with it. How do you engage with this thing that you claim is beyond your control? How do you decide that you have no merit in the face of this thing?

Now Paul is getting in the way, "Well, what if it's a big

thing—the state of economy or the state of the world?" There is
nothing that is beyond you in your attendance to yourself as an
aspect of the Creator. You must understand that you all con-
tribute to these things that you believe are so vast and so moun-
tainous. You are all in engagement with the economy, you are
all in engagement with your lives as one who proffers, expects,
calls to her what she needs to be in engagement with finance. So
if you look at your own pocketbook and you begin there, you
may attend to the world. It's a nice way to avoid responsibility,
you know, to say that "I cannot change something." Well, you
cannot change something if you don't believe you can.

Now, why do you want to be the one powerless in the face of
change? Why do you want to be the one who cannot claim her
future in the face of what has been created before you? Why do
you walk away in the face of a challenge that seems beyond you?

In this next section of the book, which we will call "The
Kingdom," and that will be the title of the chapter we are writing now, we will be taking you through your own accountability to great structure as one who can manifest the Christ in
ways that will transform everything.

Now this is not a veiled promise. When we speak of frequency, we speak of the interaction of frequency between you
and what you see before you. When you claim, "I am Word
through all that I see before me," in fact, what you are doing is
bringing the frequency and the vibration of the divine to what
you see before you, to bring it into accord with that level of
truth. So consequently there is nothing that you may perceive,

there is nothing that you may see, that you don't have power with, and choosing to deny that sets you apart from the authority that you are being gifted with in this teaching.

The moment you decide that something is too great to be transformed, you have created a false God. When enough of you decide that you have had enough of structures that favor one man over the next, that feed one man pork, feed one man fish, and feed one man grime off the floor, you will change your mind that anything can change. The aspect of you that knows who she is can perceive these things but does not know she is the one who can lift it.

Now yes, Paul, we are speaking of social change, but not in the way that you think. We are speaking of transformation on a fundamental level, that all things may be met in accord with love. As all things are met in love, all things are transported to that level of creation. And the man eating the fish reaches to the man on the floor and lifts him to dine. You all share the same air, you share the same sky, you share the same blood, the same materialization of form, so why do you hoard, and why do you hide from your responsibility to your creations? The moment you decide that the world may be healed, the world is in healing. And you will be met with the assignments you require, to do your part as one who may transform the world.

We will ask you one thing: What is the merit of this work that we ascribe to you if it is not to heal your fellows and heal your world? What is the benefit of making claims of worth—so you may get a better car? Have a happier life? You may have those things if you care for them, but they are beside the point.

You all live in a plane, in a shared experience, that you are all co-creating, and the manifestation of God as you, the expression of Spirit through you, requires you to attend to the physical forms that have been made so at this level of frequency. Everything must be attended to in conscious thought and vibration. You do not pick away a mountain with a toothpick. You do not move a boulder with a finger. When a structure has been made solid and you believe it to be permanent, you must attend to it through your vibration.

Here is what we mean: You know something to be true, because you inherit it as such. Consequently, it is a mountain; something that you must not say can be changed without appearing mad. Well, we will tell you, when we said, "Anything is possible," this is what we are attending to. The manifestations you see, each and every one of you, that are not in accord with love and were born in fear, or a desire to control, must be met in an awareness of your own divine worth. As we have said to you each, as we lift you in vibration, you call to you the expressions that exist in the higher levels of knowing. You may live your life in very different ways than you were told that you would, but you are still responsible for the creations you see before you.

So yes, while it is true that you may lift to a level of knowing and accord where you are not stuck by the rocks in the battle because you have lifted beyond them, as long as the battle is in your sight you must attend to it. What you see before you, you are in accord with. What you know to be true, you claim to be true and you interact with as true. What you say cannot be moved will not be moved.

Now, how do you attend to these things, to these structures, that would attend to you and claim their power over you? We will tell you: "I know who I am, I know what I am, I know how I serve." As you claim your authority as a manifestation of the Creator and you perceive the thing before you as it truly is, a creation of consciousness, you may change your mind, and consequently transform your relationship to this thing. If somebody tells you something cannot be healed, or cannot be transformed, or cannot be liberated, in fact, they are in idolatry.

Now Paul is interrupting, "But there are physical laws that we attend to," and yes, there are. There will be one day when no one who holds this book in their hands will be in the bodies they know now. They will have left them and attended to a new one, or aligned to a level of frequency where bodies are no longer very necessary. But as you attend to the life you live, you must understand that you have gone into agreement with the dictates that you have been told were so. The questioning, we say, is a good help but only because it allows you to take the step that we taught you earlier: "Anything is possible and will be transformed as I meet it in recognition of my true nature."

When one man stands beside a fire and blows air to extinguish the flame, it may work if it is a candlewick. When ten people surround a bonfire and blow with their mouths, they may move the flames but they may also call a hundred more people to them and extinguish the flame in another way. You all have responsibility to your environment, you share the same air, you drink the same water, and you don't act as if you are in a shared vibration. The moment you call your fellows to you, "I am Word through all that I see before me," you anchor the vibration and align to the vibration in all that you see before you, and all that you see before you meets you in this same way.

How you live your lives collectively will be what changes in the years to come. You are all having to rediscover the brotherhood of man, and you are all having to discover the inherent divinity in all things. The massive change that will occur on this plane in time will be the remembrance of love as the only truth that may be attended to.

Now, what does this look like? Well, when it happens, you will know. Will it happen in your lifetime? No. It is the trajectory of the species to move into recognition of divinity. The anchoring that each one of you reading this text is progressing with is not only for you but for all mankind. While you live your lives here in accelerated vibration, you lift the vibration of everything before you, and everything before you becomes new in your own perception. As matter transforms in the face of this—and we will give you an example of what we mean: A structure that is built in high vibration will be built in love and, consequently, will be in accord with love—the manifestation on this plane moves into alignment with what we speak of.

The Divine Self that you are is the demarcation, the response, and the requirement for all of these things to occur. You are more than a pebble on a beach; you are an aspect of the divine. And as the beach is transformed by your knowing of this, your alignment transforms, and the witnessing of God in all things will be made known to you through your own ideals, creations, and alignment.

Now, what do you need to know? "How do I embark on a new journey in this awareness of my worth?" "How do I sing my song in the face of challenge?" "How do I trust this new awareness that I am coming to?" That is what we will attend to now as we continue our teaching.

The fear of being trusted by others is a direct reflection of your fear of trusting yourself, and your fear of trusting your Creator is another way that you out-picture this. How can you trust God when you do not trust the self that is in relationship to God? Well, we will tell you. Align to the possibility, please, that the God that you know has more power than you do to teach you what you need to learn, and the God within you, the Christ as you, is the finest teacher you will ever have.

When you are confronted with something that you do not like, you must attend to it in one way or another. How you attend to your issues is always in direct accord with how you feel about yourself, what you believe you may do, and what you are allowed to change. We have already told you anything is possible. But we will tell you this: Your own need to control your circumstances is one of the things we would like to speak to.

When you are challenged by something, in many ways you are being addressed with an opportunity for transformation. And the first occurrence to each of you is to restore the balance to what you have once known, what you believe to be your safety, what you believe to be your lives. When you are a ship and you are caught in a storm, you do what you can to stay afloat, and this is understood. You do wait for the waters to stop rolling. But when you find yourself adrift on a new shore that the storm has brought you to, you may discover wonder in a way you never would have had you stayed your course.

So understand, each of you, that the challenges you call to yourself, in many ways, are re-creating your destiny for you. Now, is this a good thing, or not? You must ask yourself what you mean by that question. If you think "good" is knowing what you've known, it may not be good at all. If you know that everything you call to you is an opportunity to know yourself in a new way, you align to the possibilities brought to you by each circumstance. If somebody calls you a name, your first impulse will be to defend the self. Your first impulse may be to fight back. But perhaps the name you are called is a true name. Perhaps there is something you need to attend to in how you hold yourself to yourself that may now be addressed. You may have missed an opportunity that was granted to you in a way you didn't know.

When you decide in advance how things are supposed to unfold and you get what you want, you are quite content. But the creations that you bring to yourself this way are in alignment with a vibration that may not be as high as what is available to you. When you are in line with your own divine nature, your expression is calling to you those things that you need to know in order to progress and continue the rising in consciousness that you are attending to now. So every circumstance that is unknown to you may be the very thing that sings your future name, that will show you who you have become in your worth as the one who is attending to change.

Now ask yourself this: When was there a challenge that you have encountered that you could not endure? None of you have had an encounter that you could not endure because you are all still here. But many of you have had experiences that you believe have claimed you, have overridden your free will, and for the life of you, you do not see the benefit of them.

As we have said, every opportunity is an opportunity for you to know yourself in a new way. And in the face of pain, you may know yourself in strength. In the face of loss, you may know yourself as gifted; in the face of death, you may know yourself as alive. You may claim the things that your expression will align to. We do not tell you to be in shame for anything you have experienced. To hide your face from the light is to hide your face from Source, and Source knows who you are anyway.

The life that you would live in accord with worth does not

hold the vibration of shame. It cannot be known at this level of being. Now, the amplitude of your vibration goes well beyond yourself and the challenges you face individually. The challenges that you face individually are in accord with your individual learning needs. The challenges that you face collectively are things that you need to attend to on global realization of who and what you all are to one another. So we want to begin work on this today.

We would like you to sit where you sit and to claim your identity: "I know who I am, I know what I am, I know how I serve." And we would like you to look at the room around you, look at each thing that is there in the room, and claim this before you: "I am Word through all that I see before me," and let your alignment, in high vibration, align to everything in the room.

Now we would like you to take it a step further, and "I am Word through the home I live in," will be your claim. To vibrate as the Word through the structure that you are standing in, that you walk around in every day, and feel the vibration around you begin to extend. Now do your community: "I am Word through the community I live in—the township—the state—the country—the globe." And as you expand, "I am Word through all that I see before me," you begin to bring the frequency of the divine to bear on all things.

We would like you each to do this once a day as you learn your own vibration. You are not only healing yourself, you are bringing the vibration of the Word to all that you see before you, and you are moving beyond your personal experience to global transformation.

Now what do you say to the man that says, "This cannot be so?" What do you say to the woman who says, "This cannot be real?" What do you say to the aspect of the self that wants to go into agreement with this? We will give you the answer: Anything is possible. Anything may be claimed. And your vibration, as we have said, in accordance with God, is a mastery.

> "I am witnessing God in all the creations I see before me.
> There is nothing that I would exclude, that I would name
> as outside of God. There is no structure, there is no thing,
> that I would claim unworthy of love."

And as you lift this, you lift your vibration, you lift your world, and you live a life in accordance with your own wisdom as the one who may know the kingdom.

We will stop now. We will continue soon. Thank you for your presence. Stop now, please.

Day Twenty

We respect each of you to decide what you need. And how you act upon those needs, how you move yourselves forward to claim your lives, will be the teaching of the morning.

As you are in the kingdom, as you enter into a new realm of

your own experience of your lives, you are cautioned about one thing: fooling the self, deceiving the self, and pretending that the things that you want are in accordance with the divine will. Now, if you want a ham sandwich, by all means have a ham sandwich. But if you decide for another, and you make a claim on them, "I am seeing this for you, I am inheriting your kingdom for you, I will tell you what you are as I *wish* to perceive you," you are in false teaching.

Now we must explain this. When you witness someone before you and you see them in their worth, you are seeing them in their truth. Unless you decide to change the channel of your broadcast to acquire information for them, to support them in their development, and you are acting in that honor, you may know that you may only choose to direct your fellows in accordance with their own free will. And the support of them by holding them in truth is what will make this so.

Now when you decide for another, "She should wear that dress, she looks very nice in that dress," you are in your opinion. She may hate that dress. When you say to your child, "He should go to this school, it is a very fine school, he will be successful if he goes to this school," you are operating from your own needs. You are deciding, on your child's behalf, how he will be of the most benefit to the world that he lives in by prescribing for him the methods that you have achieved success through, or would have wished to.

Now when your child is very small, you are responsible for the choices he makes. But when the child has grown into his own awareness of what he requires to develop, your responsibility is to lead him in love, to teach him in love, to show her the way to her own self-worth and divine regard of who and what she is.

Now Paul is asking, "What if you have a child that doesn't believe any of this?" Then that is your child's right. It does not stop you, it does not stop any of you, from witnessing the worth and the inherent divinity of another. If you make everybody sit down at the table and try to convince them that they are the Word, they will all leave the table very quickly, and probably for a very good reason. You are deciding to impose your will and, if you are very excited about our teaching, you may wish to share it, but there is a grand difference between an intellectual knowing and an experiential one.

Many of you who know our work have been attended to by the frequency of the texts that we render. Part of our responsibility, as we work through the channel, is to make sure the vibration of our teaching may be presented to you in a way you may have an experience of. Part of this experience, yes, is in the intellect. You have to filter the information; it must be done in words that you may know. If we spoke in a language you did not know, you would not understand. The language that we impress upon you, we will say, is a language of light, and that is not in the page, in the sentences, it is informing the sentences, it is informing the words, and the paragraphs, and the chapters, and the entirety of the whole. As we operate in frequency, we support you as doing the same. So the consciousness shift that you are being attended to with is in your vibratory field.

When you are teaching another through language only, through ideas only, you are having an exchange of the mind. When you have an expression that is your emanation, your broadcast that they may be attended to through, you are teaching them in divine ways.

The anchoring of the Word through each of you, which we have already attended to, grants you the frequency and the broadcast to attend to all that you see before you. That does not disqualify you from other teachings, other methods of learning, but it is a way for all to be attended to in an experiential way. And an experiential way, we say, claims you in your own knowing as the one who has experienced it. It is very different, you know, than saying, "I hear the sun is hot," than feeling the sun's rays upon your skin. And that is what we offer you here.

If you wish to attend to your fellows as this frequency, there are things that we have taught you that you must attend to. You do not meet your fellow in a judgment, or a requirement that you would impose upon her. "She will be healed of that malady because I am the Word and I say so!" is your ego. "I will see the one before me in divine order, in recognition of her worth, and I will claim, 'I am Word through the one I see before me,'" will claim the one before you in divine order, and in her own purview as the one who chooses her life. You do not make decisions for your fellows. You make decisions for yourself.

Now you may choose to witness your fellows. When you see

a young man who is frightened of achieving, you may witness the young man in his ability to achieve, in his willingness to release those aspects of the self that have hindered his progress, but you do not tell him what to do. For all you know, his path may be revealed to him in an amazing way and would have nothing to do with your prescriptions for him.

You all like to decide for your fellows, "We know better," "They don't know much," and that is another way of disorganizing the news that we are broadcasting to you. Regardless of what you have done, what he or she has done, regardless of what you've believed, you are still the same stuff. And moving into the recognition of this, moving into parity of vibratory frequency, supports all in lifting.

You do not decide for your fellow what she will have for dinner unless you invited her to dinner and are offering to cook. It is none of your business what she wears, or who she loves, or how she manifests her life. You may disapprove, you may disagree, but you do not judge, and you do not decide for another.

The languishing you do, "If I could have, if I could have, if I could have," are ways of keeping you safe. When you begin to claim, "I can, I can, I can," you align to possibility. The greatest gift you can give your fellows is the demonstration of yourself as the one in her worth acclimating her consciousness to the worth in all you see before you. You are a song that can be heard, and the notes of the song will extend far beyond your reach, and inform the noise, the tone, the sound of this plane, so that others may hear and call to themselves the same truth:

"I am knowing myself as an aspect of the Creator manifested in form. And as I know this to be true for me, I know it is true for all, regardless of what I think they should have for dinner." Do you understand this?

Now we use an easy example for you, but if you look at the structures that exist that tell people who they are or what they should be, you will see the level of contamination that is informing your consciousness, and ninety percent of it, easily, is completely unconscious. It is born in history.

Now, releasing the history of being told who and what you are in small ways is a grand undertaking. But we undertake it because we know it can be so. But we do not do the entire frequency of this plane to move it into accord, we do it through the individuals who constitute the frequency of this plane, because free will is the requirement for all of you to know who you are.

You have been told many things, and much of what you have been taught has been a lie. You were told you would burn if you were one way or another. You were told you would succeed if you did one thing or another. You created class systems and ways of warring, and every one of these things has had mounds of paper to justify it. Behind mounds of paper justifying all atrocity is a consciousness that is informing it. And that is the consciousness we are speaking of now: deceit and fear.

The consciousness of deceit, which aligns to fear, would crawl beneath you and pull the rug from you, and then tell you you are better off on your fanny than on your feet. That you are better giving your power to your government than claiming it for yourself, and better to align to a church who will save you, than a God that will love you personally. There is nothing wrong with a church, there is nothing wrong with a government. These are structures. It is what informs them, and what informs you in exchange with a government, or in exchange with a church, that must now be attended to.

When you are being deceived, the window frame that you look through is being covered. It is being covered, intentionally, to filter your experience, to lower your vibration. And as you are all operating with the same filters that you have all been agreed to throughout time, you have a distorted view of who and what you are, and who your fellows are. Imagine that the window before you is encrusted with history, the blood of old wars, the tapers from old candles, the spit of old disdain. Can you imagine what it's like to look at that window and believe that to be the truth? That is what you have done.

So today, we do something new. We clean the window. And one day, we say, there will be no window at all. The cleaning of the window, we say, is an exercise in decision-making and claiming power back from the need to acquiesce to external authority that would shame you, teach you wrongly, deceive you in your merit, and claim you are something that you are not. And anything that you are that is not in alignment with your worth as an aspect of the Creator in form is a limited structure.

Imagine before you right now there is a window. And the

window is full of grime, and pain, and dirt. It folds over on itself and creates a warped view of the world. Now you will say
these words:

> "I am the one in choice. And I set this intention to clear the
> mirror before me, clear the window before me, so that all
> that I may see will be in its true reflection. And the Christ
> I see before me, the awakened worth in all men and women,
> is the cleanser I require. As I make this claim, I see all with
> the eyes of the Christ. I give myself permission to rise, to
> escalate beyond the structures that have claimed me his-
> torically and distorted my sight. I see in my worth, and I
> see the worth of all I see before me."

Paul is seeing himself before this window, as if the window is in
a rainstorm. The water pours down, cleansing the dust, cleansing the memory of shame, cleansing the debris of authority and
history from the pane before him. As he sees this happen, he
reaches out a hand to press it against the glass. And what he
will discover is that the glass itself is illusory. The separation
that you have believed existed between you and your fellows
and you and your God was deceit itself.

The Christ that you are, the manifestation of God that each
man is, each woman is, each being is, is here to be witnessed by
you. The moment you decide for your fellows who and what
she should be, you must know, once again, you are in deceit
and you are dirtying the window of your perception. The

Christ as you, we say—and we would remind you of this—the Christ as you operates as you, you do not operate as the Christ. The difference between these things is quite large, and the ego will take the opportunity to distort any teaching to fit the parameters of the frame it would like to hold.

Jesus was a teacher. He was the son of the Creator. There have been other sons of the Creator that have demonstrated the level of mastery, and wisdom, and worth and alignment to love that was demonstrated by him. He came to show the way, yes, not to be prayed to, but to be followed as an example of love incarnate.

Do not make a religion of a teaching. A religion needs money, it needs buildings, it needs to find ways to sustain itself. You do not need a religion now. You need to be in witness of the kingdom that lies before you.

We do not close your churches. There is much love in many a church. We do not seal your governments. There is much to be trusted in leadership when leadership is done in love. We come to call you out, to the town square as it were, as many of you as we can call at one time, so that you may sing the song together, and the song that you sing transforms the world you live in. What was created in fear will not hold at a high vibration. What was left in deceit to be disguised as truth will be seen for what it truly is: an operation of control, and something insignificant, we say, in the face of love.

Now imagine that you are in a town square with many of

your fellows. All the students of this text, all the students of love and worth, regardless of the text they attend to. Imagine that you all gather as one. An army, if you like. But not an army that battles, an army that sings. And you gather with a hundred, and a thousand, and tens of thousands, and you stand side by side and you witness the beauty in your fellows and you praise them in their worth:

"I know who you are! I know what you are! I know how you serve!"

And you sing the song together:

"I am Word through all that I see before me! And I will sing the praises of the Creator made manifest in all things! I know who I am. I know what I am. I know how I serve."

As you do this as one, you lift the vibration of this plane. The song will echo around the globe. And what will be heard, what will be responded to, is a kiss from all. You will feel it in your own way. You will feel your energy field align to love and the recognition of what you have just done: attended to your fellows and claimed the world before you:

"I know what you are, how you serve, and I know what you can be as you awaken to your own worth."

Since we have gathered you all in the square on a higher level of consciousness, which is what is actually happening right now, we can do an exercise with you as a group. We would like you all to say these words aloud as you attend to the book in your hand:

> "I claim my power from the passions of the fear that I have known as myself. I claim my power back from the need to control my fellows. And I release the need to be the one in charge of others' will. As I am free, I know you are all free. And as we are all free, we may choose, we may sing, and we may know."

We will thank you each for the time this morning. We have been productive. This is the end of the chapter. We will resume again in the morning. Thank you each for your presence and good night. Stop now, please.

ELEVEN

TRUTH AND KNOWING

Day Twenty-One

We ask each of you to decide something now: to pray for yourselves to be in honesty, to align to your own honesty in all ways in your life.

When you lie, you are defending something. When you are defending something, you are afraid. When you are not honest, you are out of alignment with your worth. You must ask yourself these things: "Why must I protect myself from the opinions of others?" "Why do I care what they think?" "Why do I claim my power in ways that may not be true so I may be perceived as one that I am not?"

You all believe yourselves to be so small still that you create structures to elevate yourselves, and the higher you climb on this structure without any real foundation, the higher your regard is for what could happen to you if you fall. We will tell you one thing: When you build a foundation in manifestation in your own divine worth, you are on solid ground, you have a foundation, which will hold you in all circumstances. You have a rock, if you wish, of safety, and a place to stand in your own worth regardless of what happens around you.

When you are frightened of others, you are frightened of yourself, and you believe yourself to be in jeopardy. When you believe yourself in jeopardy, you create a structure to defend the self, and the defenses you have used up until now have created much calamity. So we are offering you the new option of rising in frequency to a level of awareness where those structures are no longer required. This is world work, yes, but it happens in the individual, and as the individual claims his safety on bedrock, in a knowledge of his self-worth, and the worth of the ones before him, the alignment on this plane begins to transform. When you invest in fear, you claim fear. That is the account you hold. When you invest money in a bank, you take your own money out with interest, and the same is true with fear. When you invest in worth, you build in worth, and that is what you stand upon.

Now, when you are frightened of yourself, you make decisions born in fear and, as we have expressed earlier, every choice you make in fear calls to you more fear. And every time you call more fear to you, you create the need to defend, to lie, or to cheat. The man who knows he has what he needs does not pick the pocket of the one beside him. The one who knows the worth of his song does not try to imitate the one beside her, she knows the song herself, and she is pleased with the sound of her voice. The one who claims his wisdom as a knowing has no need to be proven right, because he already knows. Do you understand what we are teaching you now?

As you move into your own claim, "I am worthy of what I say I am," your claim is manifested before you. When you are in your worth, you speak the truth, there is no need not to.

Now, demanding others to be who you want them to be is born in fear, the need to control, the need to decide for another. When you release that need and all move into their rightful place, their own ability to choose, the world begins to rebalance. As one knows himself worthy of his choices, he knows the next man must be as well, regardless of what he presents before him.

Now what is your obligation to your fellows if you are not the one controlling them? When you are a teacher, you are empowering others to learn so that they may do their own work. When you are picking flowers and putting them in a vase for others to smell and share, you are allowing others to benefit from your choice to do this. When you are the Word, in many ways, you are both the teacher and the fragrance of the flower that emits from you. If you can imagine, right away, that there is a level of conversation happening between us and you, the reader, beyond anything you know in your conscious mind, you can understand that communication can bypass the limited ways you have understood it.

As you are manifested, "I am Word," you have claimed authority, dominion, and created the vortex for your own energy field to spin, and to heal, and to say "Yes, yes, yes, yes, yes" to each one who is before you to realign them to their own regard, and this is done without language. It is the intent. Your vibration is the teacher, and your life, in many ways, becomes your example.

Now what does it mean to live a life of example? It does not mean to behave. And that is what you were all taught. Behaving is well and good. If you are in a public place and you decide to throw your dinner plate across the room, they would be wise to escort you to the door. But the belief in behaving, in many ways, is a belief in acclimating to cultural norms, societal needs of control.

If you want to go to work tomorrow wearing a funny hat, you may elect to do that. But that very thought, for most of you, is quite nervous-making. "Why would I want to do that? I don't want to be drawing attention to myself as different. I will subjugate my individuality, and I will do what I am expected to do." Behavior, we say, is simply another way that you express yourself.

When you have agreements about what is required in certain situations, you may elect to go into agreement. It is a nice thing to bring a gift to a party if you have the funds for the gift. If you don't have the funds for the gift, why should you feel ashamed that you don't bring a present to the birthday?

We will tell you this: As you have acclimated to societal norms, you have given permission to yourselves to deny the richness of your worth and how you might be expressed outside of the paradigm of good behavior. Good behavior is agreement to a norm. Bad behavior is defying the norm. And those two poles, in their extremes, create a border that you become frightened to cross. Now when you understand that being in your worth requires you, and we underline *requires* you, to be expressed in your fullness, you must keep an eye on what you have been taught and see where you begin to deny your worth to behave, to support behavior that was invested in by others that you have used to create a frame in limitation.

"What is a good example?" Paul is asking. We will tell you. "I would love to be a farmer. My father is a lawyer. I will not be a farmer. I will go to work. I am acclimating to the behavior that is expected of me." "I am at a party. I am having a terrible time. I am supposed to be laughing. I am laughing. And I am lying to everyone." You make these choices, you see, in small ways and in large ways, and as you invest in them, they become solid structures that you then exist in.

The example that we would like you to be is as the one who is her own free will, who stands in her glory in all her choices, and claims her freedom in the face of prescribed behavior. This does not mean you defy it. This means that you know when you are attending to it and when you wish to leave it behind.

To be an honest woman, we say, requires that you tell yourself the truth. And if you are not telling yourself the truth, you will not be living a life that is truthful. How do you transform those aspects of yourself that would lie to you, keep you in deceit from your worth, and keep you back where you have known?

We are encountering Paul now, who is saying these things in his own mind: "What if I don't know where I deceive the self? What if I am in unconscious behavior?" Well, you all are, in many ways, and that is why we are teaching you this now.

The claim of worth calls all things before you. When you claim your worth and you put your hands in your pocket to pull out what you have claimed, you will see the funds in the pocket, those things that are invested in worth, and you will also see the old, those things that cannot be shared, that are unworthy, that may be fearful to you. When you have an unconscious behavior, it is informing things you do not see. You only see the results of the work of it on that life you live before you.

Now we will ask you this: Are you willing to align to your truth as the one who speaks the truth, expresses the truth, and stands in the truth in all ways? Are you willing to release those aspects of the self that have aligned to deceit and fear in unconscious ways, so that they may be brought forward and seen for that they are: creations born in fear, things that were needed at one time to support you that are no longer in alignment with your truth? If you say, "Yes, I am willing to stand in my worth, in my truth, as the one who speaks her knowing in honesty," you will be attended to now.

Imagine that you are standing on a road and before you is a bus coming toward you. The first thing you wish to do is to step aside and let the bus pass you by. That is avoidance. Now we will tell you this: What you see coming before you is not a bus, it is a lie that you have invested in, that you have invested in power, and that you seek to avoid. Your first impulse is to step aside, deny that it is there, and protect yourself from the impact.

Now we would like you to stand in the road and let this thing come before you, this fearful lie that you have claimed and hidden. Let it be seen before you for what it is: a manifestation of consciousness born in lower vibration. We do not wish you to shirk it, we don't want you to run in the other direction, we want you to stand there and let it proceed. It's not going to hammer you to the road. It is not going to crush you beneath it. It is going to stop an inch before you so that you may stand and face it.

See the creation before you, whatever you have invested in, as a big mass of unconscious junk that has claimed itself as an aspect of you that is seeking to control aspects of your life. Face this thing before you and claim these words:

"I am now the one in choice to align to myself as the one claiming power of all aspects of myself. And I give permission to release the need to invest in any behavior, born in deceit, conscious or unconscious, that may wish to claim me. I see myself as the one facing my fear without regard to what could happen, in the knowing that I am safe on this foundation I have built in worth. And as I stand here, I see this thing before me begin to realign to light. I see this thing before me as a frequency, and nothing more. I see this thing before me as a creation, and nothing more. I understand that the requirement for this thing was once born in my history, but I allow myself now to be liberated from its mask."

Everything you know in responsibility to this claim will be released, as it is required to.

"I know who I am, I know what I am, I know how I serve."

Now we will let this thing release, as it is allowed, as you align to this claim of creation:

"I am free of this thing before me. I am free of the fear I have projected outward. And as I walk forward on my path, I am no longer aligned to the energy of deceit and deceit of self that I have ascribed power to."

Now you look before you on this path and you take your steps in an acknowledgment that you are in truth, you are in truth, you are in truth.

Now freedom, we say, is freedom from fear. And true freedom, we say, is the knowing that you always have a choice. And the choice that we offer you now is to make a claim for yourselves that you may be in your merit, and you may be standing in your knowing as the one who claims the kingdom. The one who claims the kingdom knows she is the one creating in accord with her own higher knowing. The one who claims the kingdom does not see herself as victimized by circumstance. The one who claims the kingdom knows she is a way-shower as her vibration emanates, and projects and calls others to her in her knowing of who and what she is.

The example that you become at this level of frequency is manifested in this plane and the next. And by the next, we mean in higher frequency. You are existing in the heavens, you are existing on the earth, you know who you are in your infinite self, but you are aligned to the physical world that you live in so you may support it in its transition. Now is this so? Of course it is so. But can you know it? Yes, you can know it.

We want you to stand someplace today, anyplace you like, where there are people around you, where you can see them, even from a distance. And we want you to feel your feet on the ground and go into radiance:

> "I am Word through my body, Word I am Word.
> I am Word through my vibration, Word I am Word.
> I am Word through my knowing of myself as Word.
> I am Word through all that I see before me."

And feel your emanation expand to see all those things in alignment with the truth of who you are. The experience of this, and what you call back to you as a response to the experience, is what you need to begin to trust what you have chosen. You are the action of the Creator manifested in form, and the Word, we have always said, is the energy of the Creator in action.

When you tell a lie, you abnegate this aspect of yourself. You misalign it. You are trying to get away with something. When you pretend, or you want to be something you are not, you are denying who you are.

Now Paul is asking, "But isn't it true we have to see ourselves in a perfected state in order to claim that as so?" That is absolutely true, but you must understand, you are in a perfected state in higher frequency and this is what you are aligning to! We do not make you what you are not. We make you what you are!

The lie is that you are not this thing that can be made manifest in your own expression and experience. The lie is that you are not allowed, and the lie has been gifted to you for so very long that you want to call it to you again as a way of knowing yourself. We are making you misbehave—do you understand that? Well, "making" is the wrong word, but "encouraging" is the right one, if the misbehavior is about moving into truth, claiming your worth, and leaving behind the structures that would claim you in smallness, in self-deceit, and in control.

The asking we have for you now is to make decisions. "How do I know what I am when I don't want to know it?" "When I want to fight with my girlfriend?" "When I want to slam the front door?" "When I want to run away from my life?"

You must understand, each of you, that you are responsible for all of your creations. The doing of this work, while it reminds you of your choice, does not take away your responsibility. You may still pay your bills, you may still go to work, but as you continue to align your vibration and know who and what you are, your circumstances must change to be in reflection of your vibration.

Those of you who think that this is an escape from your responsibility, and those things that you have incurred and manifested in lower vibration, are thinking the wrong thing. What it means, really, is that you are required to attend to those aspects of the self that you have projected outward in whatever form they have chosen to be in, and go into recognition of them as creations born in lower frequency. As you are realigned to higher frequency, you may attend to them then.

If you got a parking ticket, it just does not go away because you have claimed your authority and wisdom. When you are in your honesty, you attend to your history so you may clear it up, but you do not reinvest in it and the difficulties that were created. You move forward in divine order as the one who is in worth.

So we are telling you this: When you live a life of example, you are hearing yourself as you speak your words. You are listening to others as they speak as well, and you are knowing what your truth is as the words leave your mouth. When you find yourself inclined to mislead another, you must question why. "Why am I doing this? What do I need from them that may only be met in deceit, and why do I engage in this behavior?"

Once you understand that you are doing this because you are afraid and, because you are afraid, you are being asked to reinvest in fear, you will see how you are being misled in deceit and you can choose the right way, the true way, of being in response.

As we have said before in our other teachings, there is never a lie that has been spoken that was not said in fear, and that includes the white lies that you excuse as a way of protecting another. We will tell you again that speaking the truth is not a call to harm your fellows, to tell them what you think at the expense of their feelings, to do harm, or to use it to defend a position that you would like to hold. You must know that you are accountable for these creations as well.

Now we ask you only this: to be in truth. Now, how do you be in truth? Well, guess what, you align to it. You align to the vibration of truth. Paul is seeing the image of a tuning fork, a band that is vibrating before him in the resonance of truth. As he sees this, he regards it, and he goes into recognition of it. He is feeling the frequency begin to work on him to bring it into congruence with his own being.

"I am in accordance with truth. I am Word through this intention. Word I am Word"

will bring you into accordance with truth. When you align to truth, you are in the vibration of truth, and what is not in truth will no longer be with you as you, nor will you need to act upon it. The resonance of the frequency of the truth that you have claimed will become your teacher.

Now we will ask you one thing: What would it feel like, for one day, to know that you were telling the truth to all you encountered? We would like you to have this experiment today. And the first thing that you will notice is how often you do not. When you are asked how you are, you lie. When you are told something, and somebody wants something from you, and you seek to deflect the responsibility of it, you find a way to dismiss the request. Just for this day, claim only the truth and recognize that by doing so you are claiming power on the foundation that you are standing on now.

"I am speaking truth, I am in alignment with truth, and I claim myself as the one who chooses to be manifest in this way. I am Word through this intention. Word I am Word."

We will stop in a moment, but we have one more thing to tell you. When you have told the truth, you are in humility. You are not in your arrogance. And there is a difference here. You do not go out and tell the world what you think of them. That would be an act of arrogance. What you think of the world is your opinion. But to be in your truth in your true way is a humble state. You are aligning to truth as an aspect of the Creator that you are expressing through.

The real truth that you know does not boast, does not sing its own praises, nor does it intend to inflict damage. It may break down a system that was corrupt and systemized through the controlling of others. It may decide to call something forward that may be witnessed in a new way. But the intention of fear—to pretend to know what the truth is—is something you must be watchful for. To be the one who tells another who she is in a way that would control her is your ego, and that is the truth. It is not your worth, or your Divine Self, in its expression.

We understand that this is a day for many of you to have an

experience of some uncomfortability. And we would only re-mind you that claiming that you are the one in truth in all of your encounters is a way of claiming your freedom from the bondage of good behavior. It is also a way of claiming your willingness to recognize all aspects of yourself, all aspects of yourself, as worthy of love.

We will continue soon. We thank you for your presence and good night. Stop now, please.

Day Twenty-Two

Hear yourselves when you ask yourselves questions. Hear what you inquire of yourselves. "What do I want today? What am I needing now? What do I long for? What can I claim? What do I know as myself through my interactions, through what I pro-ject and call to me?" Become aware of how you ask, when you ask, and what you see, because what you see before you is what you have claimed, what you have declared as your own.

When you marry yourself in a real way, "I know who I am, I know what I am, I know how I serve," you're claiming your divinity as you, and the call to yourself will always be the call to love. Now ask yourself what it means to be in the call to love. It means that the soul that you know, the identity that you hold, is seeking recognition in love through all that she sees before her, through all that he knows and would claim into being.

We continue our chapter on truth and knowing, and we

only ask that the channel step back today because we may wish to teach him as we teach our students and his interruptions, we say, will be called into question by us.

As you know yourselves in your claim of identity, you carry your credentials, these things that you believe you know as yourselves. As you introduce yourselves to your fellows, "I am the doctor," "I am the magistrate," "I am the king of the kingdom," whatever you would claim for yourself, you are not doing for the convenience of others as much as you would expect. In fact, what you are doing is reclaiming identity in lower vibration.

Now, if you are a policeman and somebody calls, "Police," you know to attend to them, and there is nothing wrong at all with knowing what your career is, and how you identify yourself through your work. But the disruption comes at a level of knowing. Can the one who knows himself as the doctor know himself as the Christ? Can the woman who knows herself as a physicist know herself as the Christ? Can the young man who knows himself through his studies know himself in this way? Of course they can, but you must realize that the larger aspect of you, the Divine Self that is you, is larger and must claim those aspects of you that you believe are made in form and hold their credentials high. As you stand in your worth, "I know who I am, what I am, how I serve," the kingdom is yours. But the kingdom is exclusive, in some ways, and this is what we must teach you now.

When you decide that the identity that you have held is

larger than the kingdom, or must be brought to the kingdom and stay as it has known itself, you lie to yourselves. You cannot bring the bomb to the kingdom and sit on it and say, "Here is the bomb. It will continue to be the bomb." You cannot call the fears into the kingdom and say, "Here are my fears, I am protecting my fears." What you bring to the altar of your knowing, what you bring to the manifestation of the Christ as you, what you call into being in the kingdom must be in alignment with love. And if it is not in alignment with love, it has no place in this new reality, this new expression, you have moved into accord with.

Now we are not telling you that you cannot enter. You have entered, in fact. It is here already. But the lower names, even the names you would approve of and show off at a party, are simply aspects of ways in which you have known yourself and realized yourself in your inheritance. Your true inheritance, we say, the Divine Self as you, wishes to re-create and realign and resupport each aspect of you in its alignment to higher vibration. The significance of this is imperative for you to understand, because some of you will run, "Show me the door!" when you understand what we are truly saying.

You cannot pretend to be what you are not anymore. You cannot deceive yourselves anymore. "I am the one who did this" is not who you are. "I am the one who claims this" is more true. But "I am what I say I am in my knowing, in my expression, as I claim my worth," is the statement of truth you adhere to.

Those aspects of you that would seek approval, that would seek to self-identify you through frames that you have inherited, or would claim to feel good about yourselves are no longer required. The true identity, the Divine Self as you, as it realigns you, will do something to you that you will not be able to comprehend until you are in the process of it. It will relegate your history to a space that is no longer required for you to identify yourself through, and it will call your future to you in a way that you will know. What this truly means is that you are no longer who you said you were.

"I am so and so who lives at such and such a place" is a way of knowing the self, but it is not who you are. "I am the woman who gave birth to three children, and had a husband and has a job" is what you have done. It is a way of knowing yourself, but it is not who you are. As the magnificence of who you are comes into purview to be recognized by you, you will begin to question things—"Why do I want what I want? Why do I claim this or that?"—and you will realize, very quickly, that who you have become no longer requires what she has known, no longer deceives herself as the one who must feel a certain way, in a certain situation, no longer requires others to meet her through an identity that you have outgrown.

The benefit of this, we say, is true liberation. And the challenge of it, we say, is navigating the landscape in a new way when you are no longer tied to expectations that you have claimed as yourself, and for yourself, historically. When a woman begins to change, when a man begins to change, those aspects of the self that are no longer operating well will be witnessed by you, and there is no way around this. You will see the reflections you have created before you, and you will ask yourself the questions, "Why do I need this to know myself? What is the benefit of this encounter, and may I move to a level of vibration where I am no longer in accord with those aspects of myself that were created in fear?"

When you say yes to yourself at this level, "I am allowed to align to own my own identity in my own worth," and you call it to you, you may thank the old creations for what they have taught you, and you may go forward and say yes to what you would call to you next.

Now Paul is interrupting. "What about the discomfort of others? What do you say to the mother who says to her children, 'I am no longer who I thought I was'?" Well, she may say that if she likes and, in fact, her children are still her responsibility, if she is the caregiver to her children. But the realization of the self at this level of love and demonstration of divinity only gives love, so it does not terrify.

Any one of you who would use our teaching to run for the hills or shirk her responsibility is in self-deception. Now, we tell you again and again that you have choice, you have the right to leave a job, you have a right to leave a home, you have a right to do whatever you want. However, you are still responsible for the ramifications of your choices, and you do this with intention:

"As I know myself as the one claiming her worth, I know myself as the one in accord with all of her creations. As I know myself in accord with my creations, I give myself permission to align myself to the highest creations I may call to me. I understand that what I have been accountable to I will need to know in order to move forward in responsible ways."

What we are telling you here is that if you run for the hills as a way of abnegating responsibility that you have incurred, you are calling to you the same responsibility in the next situation you call to you. Until you learn a lesson in your worth, you will seek that lesson again, and somebody who does not wish to claim authority over her own creations is clearly not operating in her worth.

Now Paul is interrupting, "But what if somebody is in danger, isn't running for the hills a good thing?" That is self-preservation. That is not shirking a responsibility that was incurred. That is claiming your freedom, and your true self will know the difference any day of the week.

Now, what you have claimed up until now was born in truth and self-deceit, and this is what we mean by this: Everything that you have made, and called into form, and claimed as your own, was claimed by you at a level of responsibility that you may know was born at a time when your consciousness was operating in a certain way. So if you were deceived about true identity, and you claimed things in that identity you were claiming in your truth, they were in accord with you then, but they are not in your truth anymore because you have realigned. Those aspects of you that are no longer in congruence with you will be faced if they are required to be faced, or they will be left behind.

If you go from a cold climate where you wear a heavy coat and you walk toward the sun, you will find yourself unconsciously shedding layers of clothing as you walk toward the heat. You barely think twice. And in many ways, as you demonstrate at the level of consciousness we teach you, you are doing the same thing. Some of this, we will say, is very easy, it happens of its own accord. What challenges you, we say, are those aspects of you that you would like to hold. "I am the one who did this, I must be known for what I did." "I am the one with the degree, I must be honored for my degree." "I am the one will tell you who you are because I know better than you." These are the aspects of you that you will need to confront and reclaim in higher vibration.

The destiny for each of you now is a process of integration of the claims that you have made in the texts we are giving you. This is alchemical, in some ways. It is not done through conscious intention. The process of adjusting to a new climate is one that the body does. You don't have to think twice about breathing the air at a higher altitude. You acclimate. And as you are acclimating to our teachings, there are several things you will need to know:

You don't want to do it when it is not convenient to you.

And you must understand this: Those of you that are looking for a "convenient" teaching, "I will be Word when I feel like it," "I will claim my authority when it's convenient, when I feel like it," will be disappointed with your progress. Those of you who reclaim yourselves as the one who knows who she is, who he is, and does this with an intention to re-create yourself, re-acclimate yourself to higher frequency, are engaging in the process that you may realize with less effort.

Now we will tell you what the next thing is: fear, fear, fear, fear, fear. That is the next thing. "As I operate as my worth, I am going to encounter those aspects of my self that I know are not in their worth. I have shielded myself from these things for so long, I do not want to have to attend to them. I don't want to look at my history. I don't want to know what I have known."

We will tell you this: The fear that you are seeing out-pictured in your life is a direct result of what you have chosen, agreed to, and been aligned with through paradigms of control. The witnessing of yourself in your divine worth reclaims you outside of paradigms of control. Fear will seek to stop you, yes. It will whisper in your ear, "Do not go forward, do not witness the one before you in worth, do not decide you are free," and if you adhere to those names, "I am afraid, I am not the one in choice, I will not see," you will reclaim them again and again.

Now as you claim it, "I know who I am in my freedom, I see the ones before me in their worth, I know what I may do to change my name from a limited way of expressing myself to a way that is truthful," you know yourself and you are free. The inhibitions you have held to your own freedom will be released by you, and you will stand in your worth. The names that you would claim, "I am this, I am that, I am not worthy," will release as well, because you will have moved beyond the name-calling game. You will have realigned your vibration to a level of frequency where they can no longer attend to you.

The last thing we would tell you that will stand in your way is your own choice, your own choice to release yourself from who and what you have known yourself as. If you are not willing to do this, if you are not willing to say, "I am here as I am, as I may be reclaimed in my worth," you will stay where you are as long as you wish. However, know this please: The work that we have done with you thus far in attendance to your worth is something that is being processed by you, and just because you have this experience of yourself today does not mean it will be true tomorrow. If today you don't want to go out and bask in the sun, you may well tomorrow. In the ways we speak of, the sun is always shining, however it may not always be perceived.

As you choose your lives in your merit, as you choose your lives in your worth, you will always know where you stand by what you see before you. When there is something that is no longer operating in high frequency, you will be met with it as an opportunity to reclaim your identity in a higher way. The challenges that you call to you, we will say, will always be in accord with your needs.

When you come into a lifetime, there are certain things you decide: "I will know myself in this way or that," "I will have this experience or that." Not all is predestined, but if you can imagine that there are things you have chosen to encounter, to propel you forward, to serve as your teachers, you will not be quite so frightened in the face of great change. You will not be quite so wary when you are encountered by something that you believe you did not choose.

Now the mission you each have, the readers of our texts, the students of our work, is simply to be who and what you are in the highest vibration that you are able to align to. The being of this, we say, is what creates the trajectory and the path that you walk on. The being of this, we say, is the intention to sing the song we have chosen to share with you. The being of this, we say, is what rings the bell to call your fellows forward. You do not need a tract, a pamphlet, to hand to your brother. You do not need a saying to give to your sister, you simply need to be who you are, and the re-acclimation of your identity to your true worth will be there for you as you experience yourself in your lives, as you know yourself in your interactions, and as you claim your worth.

The freedom you each seek, the freedom of prosperity, the freedom of choice, the freedom of love is, in fact, all here but has not been claimed. The trees are filled with low-hanging fruit, but you do not reach to take them. Do you understand? We are lifting you just high enough so that you may reach for yourselves and show you how to lift yourselves to the greatest heights that you may know.

Now Paul is getting in the way: "I thought you were going to talk about me. Are you going to talk about me?" For a moment, yes. The channel has an issue of his own worthiness to serve in this fashion and, in fact, that is the key to his teaching. He would be insufferable, we think, if he thought he was chosen for some great purpose. In fact, he was not. He is in his expression as we teach through him, in many ways, because we are who you all become, we are who you all evolve to. So the expression you see before you is, in fact, your inheritance.

The beauty of this, we say, is that the channel may be the student, and the student may be learning as he is cherished by us. Now you, in many ways, those of you who engage with our words, are in the same position he is. We honor this. You all know you are here for a reason. You all believe you are chosen in some way, but chosen for what? "Chosen for what?" you ask. We will tell you what you are chosen for: to be the vehicle of the expression of the divine in the way that is true to you. How you serve is how you express, how you express is how you be, in accord with your fellows and all that you see before you.

The divinity that you hold cannot be tampered with. It is sacred. It is aligned to you, and expressing as and through you as you realize this. If you believe yourself to be different as a result of this teaching or separate from somebody else, you have deceived yourself. This, again, is a responsibility of the student to the teaching. When you believe yourself to be special, you re-create separation, and you attend to your lives as the one in separation. When you believe yourselves to be enjoined in congruence with the world before you in the highest vibration available to you, you are in accord with all that is at the level of consciousness that you have attained thus far.

Is this enlightenment we are promising you? No. That is not what we are teaching you. Enlightenment involves an awareness that you have not attained yet, and the difficulty with it is you all desire it. The awareness of being, we say, in higher consciousness will bring you there. But if you seek the destination at the cost of the process of becoming it, you miss the entire point. You are all here to learn. And as you know yourself as involved in this process, you align to your Christed Self. And in this alignment you engage in the kingdom and realization, we say, is the benefit of it. Enlightenment, we tell you, will come when you claim your knowing beyond the structure of the body that is tethered to this plane.

Now Paul is confused by this teaching. "Does that mean we will not be enlightened?" As long as you are seeking it, no. When you are *being* it, it is done. And the being of it is the teaching you have been attending to in all of our classes and all of our teachings as we say, "You are who you say you who are," and the *being* of who you are is the reclamation of the true self in Christ consciousness. As you be this, you witness. As you witness, you attend to those things that would continue to realign you to higher knowing. So yes, that is enlightenment in your *being*. But do not strive. In the striving to something, you forget to be.

Now we will stop in a moment and we would like to continue this chapter when we resume. And we will only say these words in parting: There is no one attending to this text who is not in response to it. If you wish, right now, close your eyes and feel the vibration of the words on the page. Let yourself be received by us, wherever you are. Let yourself be attended to by us, wherever you are, so you may know yourself as we know you. We are here, we are here, we are here.

Thank you each and good night. Stop now, please.

Day Twenty-Three

We are asking things of the reader so that we may move forward in this final chapter. There are two more chapters in this text, but the chapter we are on now, which has to do with your own worth in your knowing and in your claim of knowing in truth, is essential for us to progress.

Your lives, as you have known them, have been contained by teachings that were inherited by you. We have instructed you already to challenge yourself as you encounter things that you were directed to understand in certain ways. What we must attend to now is the possibility that what you may know and what you may claim as you is in congruence with truth in all ways.

Now we have said earlier that you may vibrate in accord with truth. You may claim truth, and align to it as your resonance, and as you do this, you significantly shift your own awareness out of what you have known and into what you are available to at this new level of consciousness. Now we ask you this: What do you need to attend to yourselves in a new way? What do you require to learn? And you may ask yourselves now, and we will attempt to support you in the moving forward you request.

When you ask yourself who you are, you may know yourself by name, you may know yourself in worth, you may know yourself through your reflections. What we would ask you now is that you claim the knowing of the self in truth, embodied and incarnated at this level of frequency. As you are aligned to this level of knowing, your trajectory transforms itself and you face a new reflection.

"Now what is the teaching of the day?" Paul is asking. He has heard us speak of these things before, and what we are attending to today are the individual needs of the reader as they progress forward. "Who am I in my life now? What do I claim for myself now? What may I know? What happens to the plane I exist in as I accelerate my vibration?"

The actions that you are each asked to take, each and every one of you, are significant now. The plane that you exist in is in transition, and those of you who hold the vibration of the Christ, or the vibration of the light, or the vibration of the Creator, are creating a grid in support of the evolution of this plane moving into its alignment at its next level of response to All That Is. The individuals that you are are part of this alignment. If you can imagine that you are all reaching a hand up in the air, and as you pierce the clouds with your hands, you see the hands of others waving before you. The connectivity between all of you who attend to our teaching, or any true teaching of the light, is what is here to transform this plane in material form.

Now the knowing that you have of this makes you accountable for yourself here and now. As the plane that you are in is ashift in its new vibration, you may see chaos, you may see things you don't wish to see, as you realign yourself to a visual sense of what is true, as you align your perceptions to what is beyond the bedlam, or the disorder, that you may encounter.

The rising, we say, in consciousness is not always a steady thing, nor is it always graceful. It is attended to by you, in some ways, based on your willingness to be in this process we speak of. As you are attending to yourselves, you are attending to those before you, and those before you will see and recognize the worth that you have claimed, and how your life has been transformed. The idealization of you is not what we are speaking of, the example of you is. And as you lead by example, as you claim your knowing, you follow a light that will shine and those who would follow you will be led in worth.

When you don't know who you are, you seek the reflection from others. When you don't know who you are, you ask for permission. How can you know if you are allowed if you have not asked, "Am I even here? Am I even worthy? Am I aligned to what I may know?" As you claim this, you step forward and you are responsible to all that you see before you. Dominion, we say, is the responsibility of your creations.

Now, when you live in a world that often seems to be on the brink of ending, "They have this, they can do that, the world is not safe," you reinforce the paradigm of fear. When you believe that you are teetering on the brink of disaster and there are only two ways to go, down this way or over that way, you are operating in fear. When we taught you about a precipice early in our text, we never mentioned falling off it. We spoke about lifting from it, and that is the attendance we offer you now. As we lift you, as you allow yourself to be lifted, you are re-created in your own worth as you say, "Yes."

Now, what you don't know is that the life that you live at this new level of vibration is in service to all. We will take some exception to spiritual teachings that have focused on the material as a way of knowing the self. "I must be in high demonstration, look at the fancy car I got myself." "I must be in my knowing, I knew better than the one next to me." There is nothing wrong with knowing more, there is nothing wrong with a vehicle to transport yourself through—and choose a good one—however, there is something off, quite off, in recognition of yourself as a divine being through the reflection to things. "Things" will go, one day, and you know this well. The aspect of you that is eternal seeks to realize itself through you, and to become distracted by the material gains that may be made through conscious demonstration is simply a way to avoid the real work at hand, which is your relationship to you as an aspect of the Creator manifested in form.

The world that you live in is not ending. There will be a

plane here for some time to come. The manifestations on this plane will be changing because they must change, and we will tell you this: What was created in fear, and this includes institutions, religions, belief in the sanctity of power over freedom, the sanctity of fear over love, will be re-created in high regard. The benefits of this time, for those who attend to it, will be a realignment and a new congruence to their own free will as the one who knows. And the release of the past that we have attended to will be the benefit that allows you to step forward in love.

Now as we continue today, we must address Paul, who is pacing the floor in this dictation, saying, "What is new? Give me something new," as if you have the right to direct the text. The text, we say, is of its own accord, and as we work with the reader, we respond as we can to the questions we receive from the reader as they hold the text in their hands. As we do this, and we move throughout time, we attempt to shift the dictation to those things that may be supportive of one who needs to learn. Paul, you are one, but there are many learning through this transmission, and the transmission of today, which is the close of the last chapter, is instructive to those who require it.

The choice you make to move beyond a sense of limitation invites you to a new world, a new world, we say, of new possibility. A new world, we say, of new identity, and the identity that you are choosing now, your inherited self in divine worth, is the key that you ask for to be realized.

As we work with you now in vibration, we are attempting to shift you through a passage of a need to re-create the known as

a way of knowing yourself as safe. You must understand what
we are saying now: The newness that you may encounter in
your own experience of yourselves may be enough to shatter an
illusion that the past is present still. But as this happens, some
of you will be encouraging yourselves to look backward to the
known, because the person that you thought you were may still
reside there. She does not. He does not.

The memory of who you were has a knowing, but it is not
with you today. As you have claimed your vibration and called
a new life forward to you, you have agreed to stand in your
power, and the desire to return to what you have known, to
close the book now and to release your heritage, your own
claim of divine knowing, will be attended to by you if you wish.
The asking we have for you today, "Come along, come along,
come along, stand in your freedom and claim your power as the
one who knows who she is," will always be there for you. We do
not go away. And if you believe yourself to be unready for the
passage you are undertaking, be, at least, in your honesty that
that is what you are needing: to pause, to reflect, and to decide
what is your knowing is in accord with what you need.

Now the significance of the choices that you make, each and
every one of you, as you attend to this teaching, is you become
aware of the creations before you. And the magnitude of what
has been created by others is what we will speak to now. When
you see an industry that is offering profit and enslaving its
workers, how do you attend to this? When you see a design of a
way of living that imprisons the one inside it, how do you

attend to it? How do you live a life in the call to freedom when others are in chains? How do you call yourself to freedom when you see before you injustice?

There are several things we wish to say about this now: When there is a collective agreement about how things should be, people invest in it. They invest their identity, or their time, or their recognition of worth. If what is being processed by you, what you see before you and are in agreement with, is something that is not worthy of you at this stage of development, you will recognize it first, see where you've invested, and then move beyond it to a higher vibration. What we do not recommend is that you go into arrogance and decide to pull the structure down by hand. If you have a faulty house and you attempt to pull it down by the rafters, you may well be crushed by the structure you are attempting to level.

You do not heal something by going into combat with it. You do not change something by damning it, or shaming it, or claiming it is not what it is. And what it is, we say, what any of these things are, are systems of control that you have all agreed to and, consequently, have supported.

When you stop supporting a frequency by investing in it, by no longer supporting it, you withdraw your vibration so you can align to something higher. This is the way we recommend progressing as you encounter systems and things that you believe would be in control of you. The need to burn down the house, we say, is generally born in rage, and rage, in many ways, is a byproduct of fear.

Until you are at that level of frequency when you can attend to things as they truly are—you see everything before you as a creation that may be altered as you realign your relationship to it—you will be tempted to act as the child would act, and yell and scream and demand. The knowing one has no need for these actions. She knows quite well that if it is there before her, she holds accountability to her own investment, where she has agreed to it, consciously or unconsciously. And as she attends to herself, she may be called to interact, to change the structure she has seen, or she may not. As she realigns her vibration to a higher way of being and moves out of relationship with the structure, the structure no longer attends to her.

Now Paul is saying, "Is this denial? If she doesn't pay her taxes, has she risen above her taxes, or is she inviting herself to go to jail?" We have answered this already. You are accountable for all of your creations. You do not get off the hook by realigning, but you do change your attachment. And as you change your attachment, you may realign to a new way of being where such requirements are no longer necessary.

You all pay taxes because you have all agreed to it. You have all, uniformly, gone into agreement with many, many things that you do not question. As long as you know you are in choice when you do what you do, and we will say you are always in choice of your actions, you may attend to the responsibilities that befall you in higher vibration. The knowing of this, we say, prospers you in your own ability to re-create your lives in a higher way. And that is our need for you to today, to know that you can do this beyond the theoretical and into the experiential possibility that is here for you now.

As you know yourselves through your creations, ask yourself each day what aspect of you invests in it. "Where do I need this thing that I see before me?" "How am I aligned to this belief that holds this structure up?" As you claim your freedom as the one who may know, you may know more. And we say knowing is key. But as you are silent and blind to why you do what you do, you will not know such things.

We will stop in a moment but we have a direction for the channel. For the remaining sessions, we ask him to take time before each sitting to be in prayer to be in the service of his Creator in the way that is required to support the reader on her journey, on his journey, as they engage with our words. As the vehicle of expression, you are in tune with many people, and that is an offering you have gifted yourself, that you may be the tie, or the connection, to the reader and us. We offer ourselves in service in this way, and we only ask you to offer yourself in the same.

We thank you each for your attendance today and we will stop now. Good night.

TWELVE

THE ROAD BEFORE YOU[7]

Day Twenty-Three (continued)

We will ask questions tonight about your forbearance. What will it take to keep you on a path once you have claimed it? What will stop you from shying away from your responsibilities once you have decided you are the Word? What will sing your song for you when you need your remembrance of it to call you to the next station, the next place of being, as the one who has claimed his authority, has claimed her authority? What will it take for you to say, once and for all, "I am who I say I am. I am a divine being. I have anchored the Christ frequency and I express it in all areas of my life."

Why do you fight yourselves so? You go for the run and you trip over your feet and you say, "Why did I run? I fell." You get up. You don't even see the distance that you crossed before you

---

7 This chapter was delivered while Paul was conducting his regular Thursday night group.

stumbled. The road is not always smooth. The road is not always clear. But when you know who you are and you claim yourself in your worth, you are directed forward. The frequency that you hold, each of you, through the adherence to our work with you, will surmount many issues, but you must realize that you have to change the station of your broadcast to attend to what you need.

As you continue to attend to yourselves in the ways you have known, you bypass the new opportunity to bring forward the manifestation of the Christ in frequency that would be born, would be attended to, would be witnessed, would be claimed. The anchoring of the Christ vibration as you has been our work with this text. It has been our work with these classes. It has been the recognition of you, of each one of you, as this thing, that has called us to you to say, "Don't you see yourselves? Won't you witness yourselves? And won't you come forward to be seen by all?"

The fear that you have now of the walk before you is that there is no path. "The book is closed, the class is ended. I go on to my next project, my next idea. I find something new to occupy my days," and you relegate our teaching to your history. Your vibration has been transformed through your attendance to this work. Your showing of yourself to your fellows in emanation, the frequency that you hold as you express it, is a manifestation of this. You all have had this experience, in one way or another, and still you shut the book, you end the class, and you say, "What is next?"

There are many teachings available to you all, and many have great merit. The teaching that we have offered you and will continue to, in our way, is the teaching of incarnation. It is who you are in manifestation as you stand before yourself today, not as you may be one day when the jigsaw puzzle has been all filled in, but who you are today.

Today is the only day you may know yourself as the Christ in manifestation. Today is the only day you may sing your song. Today is the only day you may see the significance of your merit as an aspect of the Creator in form. The denial of this, "Maybe on Tuesday I will be the Christ," "Maybe next lifetime I will be happy," "Maybe on Monday I will decide to see my husband in his merit, but until then I am going to be angry at him," is a way of being in lies.

You have the choice at any moment to reapply, to renegotiate your relationship to any of your creations, anything you see before you that you have agreed to. The bodies that you stand in, the jobs that you go to, the rooms that you reside in and wander through, still questioning whether you have a right to be in joy, these are all creations. What would you create next? What would the man you are, what would the woman you are, create next to glorify the truth of her being, and the glory of the kingdom that she witnesses before her?

"Well, I don't see the kingdom. I see what I had for dinner last night. I see the job I don't want to go to. I see the marriage that will never be repaired. Where is the kingdom?" The kingdom is in you, and in your perception, and in your awakened self that knows that she may transform her relationship to any-thing through the decree of "I know who I am, I know what I am, I know how I serve." In this claim you claim power, in this claim you claim choice, in this claim you claim alliance and frequency in accord with divine worth.

The associations you have and maintain to your creations, in many ways, are habitual and entrenched. And if you are willing to walk with us now, we will take you on the journey to your own knowing, to your own knowing, to your own knowing.

As you sit where you are, you may say quietly to yourself these words:

"On this night I choose to align myself into accord with my knowing in a way that I may claim and I may herald. On this night I may choose to no longer deny the aspect of myself that is in holiness in her worth, in his worth, and as I create from that knowing I enjoin with my fellows into victory, into victory, into victory."

We say this: The claim of this plane into manifestation in higher frequency is the work of this class and the work of this text. The victory, we say, is over fear, is over judgment, is over those things that you have empowered, each of you, to give you a sense of identity that was not born in your worth. Your true worth, as you know, is as an aspect of the Creator manifested in form, and all other shingles you would carry, pins you would wear, names you would choose are temporary acquisitions, temporary acquisitions that will fall away one day soon.

The lives that you live, tethered to this physical plane, are finite. You have this body this time around. You have this engagement with your fellows this time around, and the next time around, when you come back to sing some more, you have chosen a different identity to engage through. But the eternal you travels with you. She is unchanged and she knows her name.

Now, the Christ as you is not a frame. A frame is a small thing that contains your world and gives you your self-worth in a parcel you can manage. What would it feel like, we say, to expand the frame you hold beyond what you have known to include all possibilities, those things that have not been seen, those things that have not been attended to yet, as manifested on this plane?

The eyes that you see when you look in the looking glass see a vision in three-dimensional reality. You understand what you see by the frame you have chosen. As you expand your consciousness, your vision expands and you may begin to perceive what has been born in higher vibration. As you align to us, and we are your teachers, we support you in aligning your sight to the vision we hold before you. What is the new world, what is the kingdom, but God's manifestation here and now?

Now, nobody is coming down from a cloud to save you. In fact, the clouds are clearing. That which has obscured the sun will be witnessed by you each, and your awareness of yourselves, each and every one of you, as this king, as this aspect of the Creator in shared love and acknowledgment of worth, is what will be known as the Christ in manifestation on this plane.

Now, we are not religious. We do not attend your churches. We may have founded some of them once upon a time, and moved beyond that structure because we no longer attend to discipline that is born in punishment. We have no need to punish you, but you still have great need to punish yourselves for your belief in your sinful nature. The telling of you, to each of you, that you were not worthy of the kingdom and that you must earn it in supplication was a tragic mistake, because it keeps many of you from standing up and saying, "May I? I may." "May I? I may." "May I? Yes, I may." You are the one who gives yourself permission to call yourself forward. We only extended the hand.

The trials that you each face on the journey you are heading on are the ones of confrontation with your own face. And we will say this: Each one you see before you is a reflection of you, and you anoint them in the way that you perceive them. "That must be a holy man, he wears a robe," "That must be a beggar, his clothes are filthy," and you anoint them all as you perceive them. "That must be a good man, he looks like a good man." There is no such thing. Do you understand this? These are frames, ways of choosing to identify so that you may feel in control of the landscape you walk on.

Until the day that you may walk down the street and witness each one before you as a manifestation of God, you are still playing the game of pretending to be in the light. The light holds no discrimination against sex, against color, against heritage. It holds no desire to keep you apart. The light shines on all, and if you would put your fellow in darkness and say that you have the right to do that, you have created yourself as a false God. The true God, we say, and we have said, loves each equally. If you are this thing that you have been claiming you are, "I know who I am, I know what I am, I know how I serve," you will see this, in fact, in all things.

Now, is this easy? In fact, it is. It is so much easier than judging your fellows. Give it a chance. Be the Word. Be who you say you are, and do not submit to the aspect of the self that would have you run for cover, lock the door, and pretend to be the only one who knows anything. That is too tempting, you know. "My mother-in-law, she will never change! She is not love! If she is on the plane, there must be no God!" and that is your agreement, that is what you witness, that is what you claim. "My son was taken from me, that man took my son! There cannot be a God, there must be vengeance, and I will not rest until there is!"

You will not rest because you deceive yourself. You make yourself the prisoner to the one who harmed your son, and you have made him a God that can control your well-being. He is still a creation, he still has his learning, and if he cannot be redeemed, if there is a man or a woman who cannot be redeemed, then there is no grace. Do you understand this? Then there is no grace, and then you should burn this book, and put yourself aside, and pick up your weapons and do what you have always done to each other.

The time is coming when mankind will face herself, will face himself, and all of his creations. And what you will be asked to face is what was done in the name of God that was a lie, and what was done in fear in the name of defense. Do you understand these words? Until mankind realizes that he is standing beside his brother, he will want to harm another. And as long as he wants to harm another, he will create ways, and ways to deceive himself that there is no Creator who holds you all in love.

The times are approaching fast when you each make decisions about what realm of possibility you wish to attend to. The convenience of the past, "Maybe someday I will get spiritual and work on this relationship with myself," "Maybe one day I will forgive my mother," "Maybe one day I will stop fighting with the lady next door," keeps you in a convenience you can no longer afford. You are saved by yourselves through your own witnessing, through your own knowing, through the possibility that you are each of the same worth. You are damned by your differences.

Now we celebrate what is different—her beautiful hair, her beautiful eyes, his skin is different than his, and his love is different than hers in the way that it is expressed. We celebrate those differences because you are unique creations. We don't ask you to be the same. In fact, you are the same. You are all made of the same stuff. You will be here one day, you will pass into the next world, and you will respond to your fellows in the recognition of who you now know you are.

"Well, that was an interesting lifetime, wasn't it?" "We sure missed the boat that time, didn't we?" "We had a good time though, some days, yes." "Well, let's do it again. Maybe it will be fun this time."

You don't have to wait, you know, to be in freedom. You don't have to wait to forgive, nor do you have to wait to know that you are loved. We said there is grace, and grace, we say, comes when it is needed. Not always in response to a request, but the hand of the Creator, we say, has made itself known in our teaching to some of you, and will to some more as you are welcomed forward on the path you are electing to take. As we said earlier, there are ways that you will move forward, and some of you still need to be told that once you are on this path, you may maintain it regardless of what you see, regardless of any disappointments, any creations that you may still call to yourself in order to learn through. There is nothing wrong with stumbling and falling, and if you wish help to be lifted, please ask. We will lift you. And if you ask in your voice, you may have fellows beside you very quickly to assist you to your feet.

You are no longer walking alone, we say. The teaching that we are giving you in our text is being shared by many now, and what has begun to happen is that when you whisper, "May it be true?" somebody else may whisper back to you, "Yes, and I know it's so. Yes, and I know it's so. And I know it's so, because I am expressed in my worth, in this possibility that we have been taught."

The joining force of vibration of those of you who ascend in consciousness create a vibration that will call others to you, and the path, we say, will be walked by many. You are standing amongst your fellows now. You are standing with the ones you know, or whom you may know one day. You are living the lives you have chosen and will continue to choose. And the creations you have created were all born in need. You needed them, or you wouldn't have created them. So now you can walk, you can walk unattended. And we say this to you: We are before you leading the way, and we are behind you saying, "Hurry, hurry, hurry. Go meet yourself. Go meet the beautiful self that you are and have always been."

We would like you each to see before you, in your mind's eye, your perfected self, the aspect of you that holds no fear, holds no rage, holds no judgment, seeks not to harm, but seeks to love. And see her before you, see him before you, as a shining light growing and expanding, and you will say these words to that aspect of you that you witness before you: "I know who I am, I know what I am, I know how I serve," and you will receive it in every cell of your being. You are merging now with your own vibration, the holiest self that you may know. And feel yourself in worth as you are engaged in marriage with your own Divine Self. "I am here, I am here, I am here" is your claim of truth. And we say, "Yes, you are. Yes, you are. Yes, you are."

This is the end of the beginning of a chapter, yes. We will continue shortly. Thank you each, and good night. Stop now, Paul.

Day Twenty-Four

We listen to each of you at night as you ask yourself, "Why was I born? What did I come here to learn?" We watch you as you walk. We see you as you ponder your own questions, and we are coming today with an answer. The path that you seek has been laid before you, and you are walking it. There is not one man, we say, who is truly lost. There is not one woman, we say, who is truly lost. You all stand where you are at this moment in time to meet your destiny, to call it to you, to sing your song in the way that you allow yourself.

There is suffering on this plane. There are experiences you do not wish to have. We do not solve all your problems but we give you some answers and we show you that you may, of your own accord, realign your vibration to your own higher knowing, to your own inherent worth, so that your response to what you see before you moves into high regard, and the manifestations on this plane transform in accord with that.

The witnessing we have asked you to do of yourselves and of those you see before you is not a moot exercise. It is a practice. It is what we respond to in our own ideals, in our ways of seeing. A practice is something that is done. An experiment is something that happens and is learned from, but a practice is ongoing.

You will not expect to meet the divine before you without the intention to be aligned to it. It is much too easy to distract yourself from your work by attending to those things that you would like to put before you that regard you as the one in charge, "My profession," "My relationship."

The identity that you are holding now, "I know who I am, what I am, how I serve," includes all these things. But you must remember, always, what aspect of the self is operating in worth, and the Divine Self as you, which is the teaching of this text, is what is brought forward to be known in your encounters, in your obligations, in all that you are expected to do.

"Expected" to do is the correct word, in this case, because what we tell you is that as you leave your lives in the ways that you have known them, the expectations change, and the requirements of your growth, as they are placed before you for you to attend to, will support you in knowing what you need and how you need to do it.

You are being given information today on the practice of the self as you are in this incarnation. We say practice is needed as you fine-tune your radio stations to always know that the broadcast that is emitting from you is something that you have attendance to. You are not overtaken, you are not disempowered, you have the choices to re-create the self in your identity any moment of any day. "I know who I am" is always true as it is claimed as you.

The lifting that you have done thus far in accordance with this work has happened on several levels. Your vibratory field has been re-acclimated, repositioned, if you like, in a higher way, and those creations that are no longer in accord with you will be met by you. Some will lift with you; some may disband. You don't need what you think you needed. If you are packing for a trip, you don't bring the swimming pool, and all the contents of the attic, and the five cars you've owned and the two ex-lovers, and the cat. Those things are not required on this journey forward. What you do need is your integrity, what you do need is your love, and what you do need is the discipline of the practice of being in your worth.

When you are encountered by anybody who would say you are not who you say you are, "You cannot be a divine being," "You cannot be worth what you say you want," the response that will bring you the best results is to acknowledge their state of consciousness, their right to hold it, and to thank them for giving you the opportunity to reclaim yourself in high worth, in high knowing, in this exchange. Every day you meet someone that you would disregard, each one of you would, and as you disregard them, "They don't have the right to be here," "I don't want to encounter this one," you incur that same response from others.

Now the alignment that you have been gifted with in the physical self is something that we must discuss. Many of you have already become aware of frequency, and as you read our text you feel the vibration working with you. The vibration continues when the pages are closed for the simple reason that you have created a connection in the auric field to your own intention to manifest yourself at this level of incarnation. Consequently, the physical body that you stand in may have its experiences of worth, of intention, in any way the body requires.

When you need something in your body, you know how to attend to it. But how you have disregarded the physical form that you stand in will also be aware by you as something you must now attend to. The acclimation of the physical self to the Christ consciousness means that you are aligning the self in body, in spirit, to this level of incarnation. You may express it in your field in ways that you may feel and know.

Now your identity, we say, which has been the crux of this teaching, "I am in my knowing," is the biggest piece of transformation that you will be attending to, and you are the one in charge of this one. The walk before you is not a short walk. We did not give you the finish line a foot away from you. The passage, we say, the triumph of the passage has been demonstrated by you already, so you must understand that as the identity continues to acclimate to the new possibilities that we have attended to you with, you will be asking yourself questions of who and what you are. The questions you ask may be answered now, will be answered now by you as the one who may know.

The process of engagement with the Divine Self as you is one of subjugation to a higher vibration. And we use "subjugation" in a positive way. What you are doing quite simply is preparing the way for the Divine Self to be fully expressed through you, and to subjugate those aspects of the self that would be in denial of this so that they may be realigned is, indeed, a process.

Now Paul is getting alarmed, "I thought we were acclimating to these things. Subjugation sounds like suppression," and in fact, that is not what we are meaning. When the higher comes through to be expressed, those aspects of you that would defy this, that would refuse it, will, in fact, be brought before you. But if you put a handful of sand before a rainstorm, you will see that the grains will fall away, and what seemed so thick and heavy in the palm of your hand may be released without effort when brought forward in the face of a higher power.

Now the creations you have made thus far will be attended to by you in several ways. You do not leave your marriage, you do not quit your job because you read our text. You reinvest in each relationship you have in accord with your new worth, you self-identify as your Divine Self in these relationships and watch them prosper. If you find that you are no longer in alliance with what you had chosen in the past, you will support its release, and you will do so in a frequency that will support you in doing this in honor, in trust, and in alignment to your worth.

You don't have to decide today that your life must change. In fact, by the adherence to this text your life has changed, and the changes will be made known to you through your own expression. You are the vehicle of change on this plane. You are the vehicle of knowing. You are the vehicle of your own true worth as it may be expressed in your life.

The dismantling of structures, great and small, will be attended to in subsequent texts, but the passage that you are in now—our readers, our students, those of you who seek the truth, who stumbled upon this text and find some resonance with our words—your jobs, we say, are to attend to you as you know yourself, as you may be known by your fellows. The triumph of this work, we say, is in your lives, is in your expression, is in all that you may see before you as you claim yourself, "I know who I am."

When we began our text, we said this was a teaching of incarnation, how you incarnate as yourself, as your higher self, the Christed Self if you wish, the aspect of the Creator that may be realized as you. And this teaching has commenced to invite you to attend to yourself as the one who may know that she is worthy of this passage. We ask you now to devote at least ten minutes a day to the practice of being. Not deciding, not changing, but simply being as this frequency. And we will give you instructions for the practice we speak of:

When you sit by yourself, ask yourself to align to your greatest potential. Invite your own frequency to move into accord with a pillar of love that may be brought forward, in and through you, to support your frequency in its transformation. As you sit in this pillar of light, this pillar of love, you claim these words:

"I accept myself as I am. I am an aspect of the Creator in full manifestation, and I align every aspect of my being to

this truth. I know who I am, I know what I am, I know how
I serve."

And then you be. You do not think, you do not choose. You
give yourself permission only to allow yourself to be in this
vibration in accord with what you have claimed. When you rise
from your seat, you will be witnessed by yourself through your
interactions with those around you as what you have claimed,
and you will express yourself in the accord that you have chosen. You are, each one of you, here and now, incarnating in the
frequency that we choose to call the Christ. That is the gift of
this teaching for all who would attend to it, and the way has
been shown.

The violence that man holds against herself, himself, will be
witnessed by you still, but you may attend to it in a new way.
"Oh, how awful!" doesn't support anybody. But to see beyond
the structure of fear that is being attended to by your fellows,
and to witness the divine worth in all engaged in violence, in
all engaged in the perpetration of fear, will support them in
realigning to their own divine worth.

You do not make somebody strong by striking them
down. You make somebody strong by lifting them to their own
merit. You live in a world that has been so caught up in its
own self-deceit that, as each one of you clears the windowpane
to witness truth, you hold the new responsibility of lifting a
vision for the rest of your fellow man.

When you see somebody misbehaving and, yes, we will put

quotes around "misbehaving," do not judge them, witness them in their merit. Somebody must misbehave, you know, to create freedom within an existing structure. Somebody must choose to walk down a new path that has not been walked before to understand a new terrain. But as one walks, one allows others to follow.

You are being given a gift today, our reader, our student, our friend. You are being given a gift today of love. And the love that we offer you is in the pillar that you will encounter each day. It will come as you require it, and you will know its presence and you may build a relationship with it. The pillar that we give you extends to our level of dimension, and we support you in your teachings, in your expressions, in your requirements for change as we are aligning to you.

The possibilities, we say, for each of you now as emissaries of this consciousness will be made known to you through your own service. How you serve, we say, is how you are called forward to express yourself in the most perfect ways. The fear that you heal by expressing yourself in your own high regard will be your knowing of the acclimation to the choice you have made. When you are no longer operating in fear, you realize it. It is if you are no longer wearing the winter coat that you always thought you had to wear. It is as if you were always wearing the sunglasses, and now you don't have them on. You will experience yourself as free.

Now we ask you only one thing. Stay in your frequency. Stay in your claim of truth, stay in your witnessing of your fellows, and stay in your alignment as the one who may choose. This has been our instruction. We do not come and rap you on the knuckles if you don't do your homework. But if you don't do the lesson, you don't graduate to the next possibility, the next instruction that we would bring to you. And we will tell you this: We have more to teach when the students are ready to learn.

We will complete this chapter in a moment, and we will say that the title is "The Road Before You," and then we will continue with our epilogue, our postscript, our final words for those of you who seek to know something new.

We are grateful for each of you, you know. We are grateful for your attendance to our words and, more than that, we are grateful for your own willingness to attend to yourselves as an aspect of the divine. We thank you each for your presence and good night. Stop now, please.

EPILOGUE

Day Twenty-Five

We teach as we can. We recognize Paul as he sits here awaiting a transmission. "What will come? What will we say to the reader as we say goodbye? Will there be instructions for the future? Is there another text? What is to happen next?" You are what happens next. You, Paul, you, the reader, you, who engages with our words—you are what happens next.

You have been directed to an expression of yourselves in higher consciousness that may be manifested as and by you as you stand in your form, in this body you know, in these encounters you have. In the recognition of your worth, and the worth of others, you begin to see yourselves as you are intended to be. You are the Christ, you know, you are all the Christ. An aspect of you was seeded by your Creator to come into awareness of this, and our direction, our command, our gift to you, is that you awaken to your divine potential and recognize it in all the ones before you.

The sacrifices that you make as you go on this journey are the sacrifices of fear, the indulgence of fear to direct you in your actions. The sacrifices you make as you go on this journey is the fear of being realized, the fear of being the self in the worth that you can hold. The sacrifices that you make as you go on this journey are the limitations of history that you would call to you to give you a structure, a sense of self, born in what was. What is, we say, what has come forward, is you, is each of you, each one of you in recognition of your Divine Self.

We ask you only one thing: Do not deny the God in anybody else. The command that we give you here is a very important one. The moment one of you elevates yourself as a scholar, as a teacher, as a seer above the other, you create imbalance.

Somebody may climb to the top of the tree to witness the view there, to describe it to the ones below, but never at the cost of inviting them up to join him. One may stand on a mountain and decree something, "I tell you all this," but if the words are not born in love they are meant to fall on deaf ears. The one that would whisper love, the one that would challenge fear, the one that would see you all in your divinity and tell you, "Yes, you are, you are this thing you say you are," is the one to call forward and hear.

Now we will ask you: Have you questions? Have you questions still? Because your questions, we say, as you give them to us in the ethers are considered by us and we reflect upon the needs of each of our students as we continue our writings. And we will say this to Paul: You are not done yet. There is more work to do, and we are grateful for your presence as the one who can serve in this capacity for your fellows. We are the teachers, yes, but what we do with you, with Paul we say, is release him from a history of fear so that he may become a clearer transmitter and the transmission we seek to offer you may be untainted. So the worth we see in all of our readers is being witnessed by us as we see through Paul, as we hear through Paul, and as we hear your words directed outward into the fabric of All That Is.

When we reach our next book, there will be new directives, new ways of teaching born in the requirements of the students who have attended to this text, and we will seek you out and we will ask you, "Yes, how can we be of help? What may we need to know to continue our teaching?" The blooming in each of you, the awakening in each of you, is what is being attended to now. And when a flower is blooming, the fragrance is lovely. And the fragrance that you hold, we say, is the emission, the divine emission of the frequency of the Christ as you. No one is born in sin. Everybody is born into a body and into a sense of awakening.

Each day you awaken to a new world if you will let the world be new. Each day you will see your fellows anew if you will let your fellows be seen. Each day you will sing your song if you align to the song you have been instructed in. You are the chooser here. You have always been the chooser. We are giving you the keys to the car, in some ways, that you have always been driving and pointing you on the road to the highest mountain so you may know yourself from that reign, from that ability to see, from that clarity of sight that is permissible to you from the heights you may seek to rise to.

Now no one here who attends to our words is without our need to support you. There is no one who attends to these teachings who does not get seen and aligned to as you work with the vibration "I am Word." Do not get caught up, please, in the intensity of the vibration. Do not be deceived by the ability to feel energy. It does not make you special. It aligns you to your next shift. When you are being worked with at this level, and we say you are being worked with, you will come to know yourselves in different ways. But always remember, please, that the ones beside you are your brothers, they are your fellows, and you walk as one.

We do not elevate one man above another. We do not elevate one teaching above another. We simply sing, and if the song we sing is of pleasure to you, please join us now in saying these words:

"On this day I claim to know myself in my worth.
On this day I claim to know myself in my beauty.
On this day I claim to align myself to worth, to sing my
    song for the benefit of all.
I am here, I am here, I am here."

When you claim this, you call your vibration into frequency in this manifestation. The words we have gifted you with through this text, "I know who I am, I know what I am, I know how I serve," will center you, will clear you, will ground you in present time so you may claim in accordance with your worth. You have been gifted with tools, but beyond that, you have yourselves, you have your precious selves. The Divine Self that is you seeking expression as you is here, is here, is here.

Now we will ask you only this as we say good night for this text. Will you come with us on the next journey? We are already calling Paul forward to a new highway, a new witnessing of what is before him. And we do this so that he may transmit the words to you and you may come along. We will take a pause between books, but only to acclimate the vibration of the readership that is attending to this text so that she may be prepared for what is to come. And mastery, we say, will be the text we write next. "I am in my mastery."

We are honored to know you, you know, all of you who came at this time to awaken to your worth, to see one another in their beauty, and to dance as you live to the song that is now being sung in the name of the new light that has come to glow and to be as you.

We see you in your beauty
We see you in your courage
We see you in all you have known and all you will discover
    as new
We see you in what you have claimed
We see you in what you have let go of

We see you in your witnessing

We see you in your choice

We see you in your dismantling of structures

And in climbing new heights

We see you on the mountaintop waving to your fellows

We see you singing loudly so that others may be called
to you

We see you in a whisper so that others may hear your
softness

We know that you love

We know that you express

We know that you are who you say you are.

And that has been our teaching. We leave you with love, and we leave you with these words:

I am Word.

Thank you and good night. Stop now, please. Period.

ACKNOWLEDGMENTS

Tim Chambers, Beth Grossman, Mitch Horowitz, Amy Hughes, Jeannette Meek, Victoria Nelson, Dustin Parent, Alan Steinfeld, and the members of the Thursday Night Energy Group

ABOUT THE AUTHOR

Paul Selig was born in New York City. He attended New York University and received his master's degree from Yale. He had a spiritual experience in 1987 that left him clairvoyant. As a way to gain a context for what he was beginning to experience, he studied a form of energy healing. He began to "hear" for his clients, and much of his work now is a clairaudient, empath, and conscious channel. He lives in New York City where he maintains a practice as an intuitive and offers channeled workshops throughout the country. Also a noted playwright and educator, Paul directs the Master of Fine Arts in Creative Writing Program at Goddard College and teaches at New York University. His website is www.paulselig.com.

If you enjoyed this book, visit

www.tarcherbooks.com

and sign up for Tarcher's e-newsletter to receive special offers, giveaway promotions, and information on hot upcoming releases.

TARCHER
PENGUIN

Great Lives Begin with Great Ideas

Connect with the Tarcher Community

• • •

Stay in touch with favorite authors!
Enter weekly contests!
Read exclusive excerpts!
Voice your opinions!

Follow us

 Tarcher Books

@TarcherBooks

If you would like to place a bulk order of this book, call 1-800-847-5515.